ABCD Tech

Riktesh Srivastava

ABCD Tech

Revolutionizing Business with Artificial
Intelligence, Blockchain, Cloud Computing,
and Data Analytics

 Springer

Riktesh Srivastava
College of Business
City University Ajman
Ajman, United Arab Emirates

ISBN 978-981-96-4308-0   ISBN 978-981-96-4309-7   (eBook)
https://doi.org/10.1007/978-981-96-4309-7

This Springer imprint is published by the registered company Springer Nature Singapore Pte Ltd.
The registered company address is: 152 Beach Road, #21-01/04 Gateway East, Singapore 189721, Singapore

If disposing of this product, please recycle the paper.

To the visionaries and explorers who cherish technology and transformation, To the unremitting learners who view uncertainties as paving steps to progress, And to the countless unheralded champions in technology whose devotion serves the future. May this book shed light for those traversing the opaque seas of digital change, encouraging daring ideas, transformative discoveries, and a better future for everyone.

Preface

In a phase when technology is not solely an instrument but an ignition of seismic shifts, companies must continually develop to remain competitive. Artificial intelligence, blockchain, cloud computing, and data analytics—collectively known as "ABCD" technologies—are no more emergent phenomena but basic pillars altering businesses, offering new possibilities, and probing established methods.

ABCD Tech: *Revolutionizing Business with Artificial Intelligence, Blockchain, Cloud Computing, and Data Analytics* is both a detailed reference and a blueprint for traversing this unfamiliar world. This book goes deep into the revolutionary impact of these technologies, explaining their significance throughout numerous sectors while offering practical examples that exhibit their potential to create effectiveness, creativity, and progression.

The fast evolution of ABCD technologies has also encouraged an environment that fosters collaboration and development. Businesses and individuals from all corners of the world are using these technologies to construct better, more agile businesses, paving the way for a technologically connected society. Regardless of whether you are an entrepreneur, a company executive, or a tech enthusiast, the concepts in this book give a path to using new technologies for sustained, meaningful development.

This preface is a request to consider each chapter with a sense of curiosity and a willingness to reassess what is feasible. Embrace the adventure, as you examine how ABCD technologies are not only influencing business but also transforming every aspect of ourselves and culture.

Ajman, United Arab Emirates   Riktesh Srivastava

Acknowledgments

Writing this book has been an unforgettable endeavor, and I am truly thankful to everyone who helped to bring to its accomplishment.

First and foremost, I would like to publicly express my sincere appreciation to my family and friends for their constant morale and support during every step of the way. Your understanding and tolerance have been my continual drive.

Many thanks to my publisher and editor, whose orientation, competence, and perspective have given the necessary clarity to complete the book.

I am also thankful to the mentors and peers who have influenced me throughout the journey.

Your expertise and understanding have tremendously affected the thoughts and notions inside this book.

To all the readers, thank you for reading this book and going on this adventure with me. Your thirst for understanding makes this attempt relevant and rewarding.

Finally, I appreciate everyone who, directly or indirectly, has been a part of this adventure. Each of you has added to the effort in a unique and significant manner. This book is an expression of our united efforts, and I am profoundly thankful for every one of you.

Thank you.

Contents

Chapter 1
Introduction to ABCD Technologies

Abstract This chapter introduces the four disruptive technologies together known as ABCD Tech—artificial intelligence (AI), blockchain technology, cloud computing, and data analytics—and inspects their transformative effect on business operations. While each of these technologies has self-sufficiently compelled substantial developments, this book emphasizes their integration and mutual influence in boosting business efficiency, transparency, decision-making, and consumer experience. The chapter begins with an outline of ABCD Tech, providing an analysis of their core principles, applications, and contributions to business processes. AI automates tasks and personalizes consumer interactions; blockchain enhances data security and transparency; cloud computing enables scalable resource management; and data analytics summaries insights from huge datasets. The next section highlights the importance of ABCD technologies in the business, concentrating on their part in pouring efficiency, transparency, decision-making, and enriched consumer experiences. The section introduces the mathematical models that illustrate the transformative impact of ABCD Tech. Following this, the chapter explores the synergistic benefits of integrating ABCD Tech. By merging AI with data analytics, businesses can extend predictive capabilities, while blockchain and cloud computing together confirm secure and efficient data processing. A mathematical framework is introduced to assess the compounded efficiency gains resulting from this integration. Finally, the chapter concludes with business scenarios showcasing businesses that have efficaciously implemented ABCD Tech for a competitive advantage. These examples validate theoretical models and highlight the practical benefits of adopting an integrated ABCD Tech approach.

Keywords ABCD technologies · Artificial intelligence · Blockchain technology · Cloud computing · Data analytics

1.1 Introduction

The chapter explains the basics of the four disruptive technologies that are commonly used by businesses today. The four technologies are: A for artificial intelligence, B for blockchain technology, C for cloud computing, and D for data analytics (or what is called as ABCD technologies). These technologies have separately helped businesses; this book will examine how the integration of ABCD technologies is helping businesses now.

The first chapter explains the underlying fundamentals of each technology and how the business employed them independently. However, as technology expanded, businesses needed an integrated approach to use these technologies effectively. The chapter examines how integrating these technologies benefited businesses.

The chapter is divided into four sections. The first section gives a thorough overview of ABCD technologies, and explores into each technology in a comprehensive manner, providing an extensive understanding of each of these technologies and the way they influence business. The second section elaborates the transformative impact of these technologies individually on the business. The section uses the analytical concepts to explain how each of these technologies enhances efficiency, transparency, decision-making, and customer experience for the businesses. The chapter's third section addresses the integration of ABCD technologies and shows how they complement each other when integrated. The section explores further into how the integration of ABCD technologies yields synergistic advantages for businesses. The fourth and final section of the chapter gives examples of businesses that use ABCD technology to gain a competitive advantage.

1.2   Overview of ABCD Technologies

1.2.1   Artificial Intelligence

Artificial intelligence (AI) is revolutionizing businesses by automating processes and thereby improving consumer experiences. AI helps businesses harness data, learn from it, and conduct tasks that earlier required human beings (Mitchell, 2013). The four ways AI helps businesses are machine learning (ML), natural language processing (NLP), computer vision, and robotic process automation (RPA). Let's explore each of these in detail:

1.2.1.1   Machine Learning

ML is the technique where the system learns from data and helps to automate business process. ML is critical for making business decisions and helps to make predictions. A retailer can use machine learning to forecast the consumer purchase trends, thereby helping to improve consumer experience. ML algorithms use previous purchase data to assess trends, seasonal patterns, and the possibility of particular products that can be bought in the future. Amazon, for example, uses machine learning to propose products according to surfing patterns as well as purchase history (Mitchell, 2013). General Electric (GE) uses ML to forecast maintenance in its industrial equipment, by collecting data from sensors on machines thereby preventing unexpected failures (Chen et al., 2023). Also, MasterCard relies on machine learning for recognizing unauthorized transactions. PayPal and MasterCard use anomaly detection algorithms to identify strange transactions allowing real-time warnings to consumers as well as banks (M. Ahmed et al., 2015).

1.2.1.2   Natural Language Processing

NLP enables AI to perceive, interpret, and react to human language. Nowadays, many companies are using NLP for consumer service automation as well as sentiment analysis. Starbucks harness NLP to predict the consumer preferences based on consumer comments and reviews. HDFC Bank enhances the consumer experience through its Chatbot Eva, which helps to answer the queries in real time. Dubai Electricity and Water Authority (DEWA) introduced the Chatbot Rammas, which provides real-time assistance regarding bill payments, service enquiries, and issue resolution in both English and Arabic. Thus, NLP is thus used by companies in real time to converse with humans and discover reoccurring problems, answer queries and analyze customer feedback, automate routine tasks, and provide personalized recommendations(Necula, 2023; Yixuan, 2024).

1.2.1.3   Computer Vision

Computer Vision (CV) permits AI to understand and evaluate visual inputs to detect patterns, recognize faces, and analyze environments. By doing so, CV helps in facial recognition, maintaining quality control in manufacturing, and enhancing automation. In its Amazon Go stores, Amazon uses CV, where cameras and sensors analyze consumer movements to track products and automate the checkout process. Fynd, an online fashion retailer in India, uses CV, wherein the consumer can upload the picture of the cloth they want, and CV finds the similar cloth on its website. Noon, an online retailer in the UAE, uses CVs for searching. The consumer can upload a picture to locate the product on its website. Also, Tesla uses cameras and sensors to gather enough information—photographs of automotive components—and CVs identify flaws through assessing real-time images to specified quality criteria (Soori et al., 2023).

1.2.1.4   Robotic Process Automation

RPA is the application of AI that automates routine tasks such as data input, invoicing, and report preparation. Walmart uses RPA to automate its inventory management and order processing. Alibaba has also started to use RPA to automate its consumer service operations as well as inventory management. Flipkart uses RPA in its back-office work including consumer support and supply chain management. Also, Majid Ai-Futtaim, a retail company in the UAE, started to use RPA for supply chain, inventory management, and consumer service. RPA actually eliminates human labor and increases efficiency in business operations by lowering processing time and mistakes (Richey Jr. et al., 2023).

Thus, there are various scenarios in which businesses are using AI. The only impediment to AI adoption is data quality, since poor data quality leads to erroneous predictions and inefficient decision-making. When the data is clean and organized, it influences the performance and dependability of AI models. Also, with the introduction of data management and preprocessing, businesses can now receive quality data, allowing them to leverage the full potential of AI technology and make decisions with greater certainty.

1.3   Blockchain

Blockchain is a decentralized, digital ledger that records data across many computers in a way that data can't be altered or tampered with. Each data is saved in a block, and once a block becomes full, it gets linked to the chain of previous blocks, making the blockchain. Figure 1.1 shows the blockchain:

As can be seen in Fig. 1.1, a blockchain is a chain of blocks, where each block contains data. This data could be of any form (normal data or transaction record). The blocks are connected together in an ordered manner, making a chain (thus, it is called blockchain). If you see in Fig. 1.1, each block holds several important parts:

- Index: The block's place in the chain (Block 0, Block 1,...)
- Timestamp: The specific time the block was added
- Previous Hash: A unique code for the previous block in the blockchain
- Hash: The block's own distinct code
- Data: The content stored in the block

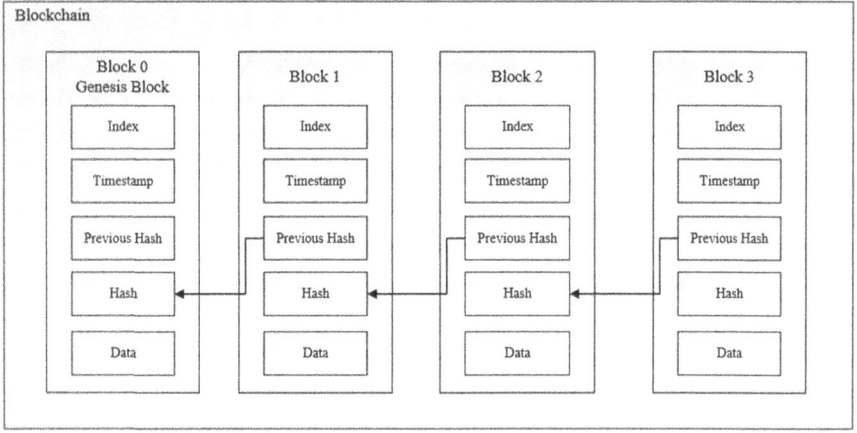

Fig. 1.1 Blockchain (Source: SphereGen, 2020)

The first block in the blockchain is called the *genesis block*. Genesis block is not connected to any previous block (since it's the first one), and also does not contain any data.

1.3.1 Properties of Blockchain

Blockchain technology possesses multiple properties that make it beneficial for businesses. Below are the six most prominent properties of blockchain:

1. *Decentralization:* As in conventional systems, where the data is controlled by central authority or intermediaries, blockchain functions on a decentralized network of nodes (computers). Every node gets access to the exact same data, eliminating the need for central authority or intermediaries.
2. *Transparency:* Every transaction on the blockchain is accessible to all participants in the network.
3. *Immutability:* Once data has been added to the blockchain, it can't be modified, edited, or erased, making it immutable.
4. *Consensus mechanisms:* Blockchain technology employs consensus mechanisms (e.g., Proof-of-Work, Proof-of-Stake) which are an agreement among the members that the transaction is legitimate.
5. *Distributed ledger:* Blockchain is a distributed ledger, with each node owning a copy of the complete chain.
6. *Smart contracts:* Some blockchains do not offer transactions; rather they offer smart contracts. Smart contracts are autonomous agreements, which automatically execute and impose actions when specific criteria are met.

1.3.2 Types of Blockchain

There are three types of blockchains used by businesses, each intended to accomplish different requirements.

1.3.2.1 Public Blockchain

A public blockchain is not owned by a single company but rather operates on a peer-to-peer network where all the nodes in the blockchain maintain a copy of the data. Thus, the public blockchain is decentralized in nature, where every piece of data is accessible to all the users in the network. For example, Walmart uses IBM's Hyperledger Fabric (a public blockchain by IBM) to track the food supply's transparency. Everledger also uses IBM's Hyperledger Fabric for diamond tracking. In finance, platforms like Uniswap and Aave use the Ethereum blockchain, which allows for direct trading and lending in the public cloud without the need of intermediaries. AXA's flight delay insurance uses smart contracts by Ethereum blockchain for insurance claims for flight delays. Additionally, Brave Browser and KickCity use the Ethereum blockchain to facilitate tokenization and crowdfunding through ICOs.

1.3.2.2 Private Blockchain

A private blockchain is a permissioned blockchain that operates in a closed network, and only the companies that are allowed can access and contribute to the blockchain. Private blockchains are used by companies for their internal operations or collaborations between partners while maintaining confidentiality. For instance, Walmart uses IBM's private blockchain to track food products from farm to its stores. JPMorgan's private blockchain Quorum is used by banks to facilitate financial transactions between banks. In healthcare, a private blockchain called the MedRec system manages sensitive patient data while also ensuring privacy for authorized providers. Deloitte's private blockchain auditing solution, called Deloitte Block Chain Auditing Solution, is used by companies like HSBC, Samsung, and Cargill for auditing purposes. Overall, private blockchains empower businesses across various sectors to improve operations, trust, and security while safeguarding sensitive information.

1.3.2.3 Hybrid Blockchain

A hybrid blockchain combines both the public and private blockchain. There are two layers in the hybrid blockchain. The first part is a public layer which is open to any user and is normally used to hold data that can be accessed by public like transaction records or product authenticity. The second part is called a private layer that is restricted to authorized participants and is used to store sensitive information like consumer data or proprietary business data. Dragonchain, the hybrid blockchain developed by Disney, allows businesses to build hybrid blockchains. It offers both public and private layers, thereby companies can use the private blockchain to keep sensitive data and use the public blockchain for data to be shared to public. XinFin is a hybrid blockchain platform for global trade and finance, and Chronicled uses a hybrid blockchain to improve the pharmaceutical supply chain. Chronicled provides a public blockchain for tracking drug compliance, while the private blockchain has the data related to contracts and pricing, which needs to be authorized for participants.

Among the three types of blockchain technology discussed, hybrid blockchain is most typically adopted by businesses owing to its balanced approach and reduced cost.

1.4   Cloud Computing

Cloud computing is like using the Internet to access and store data and applications instead of keeping everything on your personal computer or local servers. Imagine storing your photos on a service like Google Photos or using software like Microsoft Office 365 online. This way, you can access your files and applications from anywhere with an Internet connection.

1.4.1   How Businesses Use Cloud Computing

There are a number of ways businesses use cloud computing:

1. *Data storage:* Businesses store a large amount of data over cloud which can be accessed from anywhere.
2. *Software as a service (SaaS):* Businesses now use software over the Internet and thus do not need to install them on desktop. This helps businesses to save on infrastructure and access this software from anywhere providing flexibility, remote collaboration, and scalability in operations.
3. *Scalability:* Businesses are able to rapidly scale up or down the resources based on demand, ensuring they only pay for what they use, which reduces costs. This flexibility enables businesses to swiftly adjust to changing market conditions without excessively investing in infrastructure.
4. *Remote work:* Cloud services allow employees to work from anywhere, boosting freedom and productivity. This helps businesses to cut office space costs while maintaining consistency even during challenges like natural disasters. Additionally, cloud-based collaborative applications enable real-time conversation and document sharing, improving team planning and effectiveness across different time zones.

1.4.2   Properties of Cloud Computing

The properties of cloud computing for businesses include:

1. *Self-service:* Businesses can access resources as they require without any intervention from the cloud service provided.
2. *Broad network access:* Applications used can be accessed from devices such as laptops, tablets, and smartphones.
3. *Resource pooling:* Cloud service providers share resources with multiple customers, resulting in efficient resource utilization and cost savings.
4. *Rapid elasticity:* Businesses can scale up and down the resources as needed.
5. *Measured services:* The services used by businesses over the cloud can be measured and can be paid either using pay-as-you-go or subscription plans.

1.4.3   Types of Cloud Computing

There are three types of cloud computing services often used by businesses. These are:

1. *Public cloud:* In public cloud, the services and resources are provided to multiple businesses. Amazon Web Service (AWS) and Microsoft Azure are two major public cloud providers, which offer a wide range of services to customers. Netflix uses AWS for data storage and streaming services. Flipkart also uses AWS to manage the data generated from its e-commerce platform, and Careem, a ride-sharing service in the UAE, uses Azure for all of its operations.
2. *Private cloud:* Private cloud is tailored to a single business and offers greater security and control than public cloud, making them optimal for businesses with rigorous data protection and compliance requirements. These clouds can be either used by businesses to host-on-site or handled by third-party companies. For example, Bank of America uses private cloud solutions that adhere to stringent security and safety standards for dealing with financial data. Similarly, BMW uses a private cloud to manage its production procedures while safeguarding secret customer information. In China, Huawei offers private cloud options to its corporate customers, focused on security and data protection for important business processes. In India, Tata Consultancy Services (TCS) offers private cloud services to businesses in regulated sectors such as banks and healthcare, supporting them keep compliance while ensuring data security. Meanwhile, in the UAE, Etisalat features private cloud services, ensuring businesses work in a secure and controlled setting for their confidential information.
3. *Hybrid cloud:* Hybrid cloud mixes private and public cloud platforms, allowing businesses to balance between security and adaptability. For example, General Electric (GE) uses a private cloud for sensitive industrial data while using the public cloud for data analysis and processing. Infosys saves sensitive customer information in private clouds to meet regulatory requirements while employing public cloud for its development and testing purposes. Emirates NBD, in the UAE, keeps important banking data in a secure cloud, while employing the public cloud for customer-facing apps and online services. Thus, hybrid cloud allows businesses to use both private and public cloud that helps them to reduce costs and ensure data safety.

Thus, businesses use private clouds for security and control, public clouds for scale and cost-effectiveness, and hybrid clouds if they require a balance of both. But, out of the three types of cloud services, hybrid cloud is the most recommended one for businesses.

1.5 Data Analytics

Data analytics is the tool used by businesses to collect, analyze, and interpret large quantities of data. This interpretation of data (or outcomes) helps businesses discover useful information that helps them make decisions and maximize business performance.

There are a number of examples that elaborate on how businesses use data analytics. Let us explore some of them here:

1. Through a recommendation system, Amazon observes browsing behavior and makes recommendations to consumers (improving consumer experience).
2. Netflix observes viewing habits and promotes shows that align with those preferences (optimize viewing).
3. Coca-Cola collects real-time supply data and optimizes its supply chain (operational efficiency).
4. JP Morgan uses data analytics to detect the fraudulent transactions (improving financial decisions).
5. Spotify observes users' listening patterns and constantly updates its playlist (product development).

1.5.1 Properties of Data Analytics

The features of data analytics may be characterized using the seven V's, which allow businesses to comprehend and manage data:

1. *Volume*
   Volume refers to the vast volume of data created from a number of sources.
2. *Value*
   Value refers to obtaining relevant information from a big volume of data.
3. *Variety*
   The data saved might be of many types: structured (databases), semi-structured (XML), and unstructured (Social Media).
4. *Velocity*
   Velocity defines the pace at which the data is created and should be processed rapidly for successful decision-making.
5. *Veracity*
   Veracity relates to the correctness, dependability, and trustworthiness of data. High-quality data offers organizations with important insights.
6. *Variability*
   Variability refers to the changing nature of data collection across time.
7. *Visualization*
   Visualization offers the facts in a visual format that enables for easier decision-making.

Together, the seven V's underscore the complexity and potential of data analytics. Managing these features successfully helps businesses to harness their data for enhanced analysis and profitable growth.

1.5.2   Types of Data Analytics

There are four main types of data analytics that businesses use to respond to different kinds of queries and make improvements:

1. *Descriptive analytics (what happened?)*: Descriptive analytics digs into historical data to provide insights about the past performance. For example, Walmart uses past data to figure out which goods sell more during specific times in order to handle supplies effectively.
2. *Diagnostic analytics (why did it happen?)*: Diagnostic analytics explores for patterns or trends in the data. For example, Starbucks applies diagnostic analytics to assess the drop in sales and comprehend the customer taste or insignificant promotions.
3. *Predictive analytics (what will happen?)*: Predictive analytics analyzes data using complex statistical methods, along with machine learning to predict. For example, Uber uses predictive analytics to discover customer needs using the data from previous rides. Coca-Cola applies predictive analytics to anticipate future sales and handle its inventory efficiently.
4. *Prescriptive analytics (what should we do?)*: Prescriptive analytics makes recommendations based on the findings of data analysis. For example, Delta Airlines depends on prescriptive analytics to handle its flight plans based on weather estimates, previous delays, or busy trip times. Similarly, Amazon uses prescriptive analytics in their warehouse operations, where, depending on the order trends, recommendations for products in the warehouse are handled.

The most common type of data analytics employed by businesses is descriptive analytics, where the business seeks to evaluate past achievements. However, with advancements in technology (such as machine learning), predictive analytics are being used by businesses for predicting reasons. The usage of predictive analytics has continued to grow in businesses today and is widely used for strategies based on outcomes. Thus, by using the different types of data analytics (descriptive, diagnostic, predictive, or prescriptive), businesses gain useful insights and maximize their business performance.

1.6   Importance of ABCD Technologies in the Business Backdrop

ABCD technologies contribute toward business transformation. The main transformation each of the businesses gets is efficiency, transparency, decision-making, and customer experience. These transformations have played a significant role in revolutionizing the business. We will be discussing each of these transformation roles for each of the ABCD technologies.

1.6.1   Transformative Role of AI in Business

Efficiency
AI improves business efficiency by automating the repetitive tasks and optimizing business processes.

Mathematically, efficiency (E) without intervention of AI can be denoted as

$$E = \frac{N}{T} \tag{1.1}$$

where N is the number of tasks to be completed, and T is the time taken to complete the tasks.

The value of E is quite high, because the efficiency is calculated based on the repetitive tasks as well. However, with the intervention of AI,

$$E_{AI} = \frac{N}{T_{AI}} > E \tag{1.2}$$

With AI, the time T_{AI} reduces leading to increased efficiency.

Also, if all the tasks are automated, then the time taken to complete the tasks can be represented as the function of complexity of tasks C and can be given as

$$T = f(C) \;\; \rightarrow T_{AI} = f_{AI}(C) \tag{1.3}$$

As the complexity decreases because of the automation and elimination of repetitive tasks, the time taken to complete the tasks also reduces significantly. Thus, the impact of AI can be defined as:

$$E_{AI} = \frac{N}{f_{AI}(C)} > \frac{N}{f(C)} = E \tag{1.4}$$

Transparency

AI helps businesses with transparency by providing insights based on data and also by tracking data across business operations.

If T represents transparency and D are the data points available, then transparency can be represented as

$$T = f(D) \tag{1.5}$$

where function $f(D)$ defines how data gets transformed into insights for businesses.

With the intervention of AI in the business, the transparency can be denoted as:

$$T_{AI} = \int_0^D f'(d)dd \tag{1.6}$$

$f'(d)$ represents the rate of change of insights because of introduction of AI in business processes.

Decision-Making

AI helps businesses in decision-making because it helps to analyze more quality data and thus provide actionable insights.

If A be the actionable insight provided because of the quality of data, and T represents transparency, then decision-making can be represented as

$$D = g(A, T) \tag{1.7}$$

where $g(A, T)$ is the function of both accuracy and transparency.

Because of introduction of AI, the decision-making can be now given as:

$$D_{AI} = \int_0^A g'(a, T_{AI})da \tag{1.8}$$

$g'(a, T_{AI})$ is the rate of change of decision quality due to AI.

Customer Experience

AI helps to improve customer experience due to personalization; thereby customers are more engaged and satisfied.

If C represents customer experience and P is the level of personalization, then

$$C = h(P) \tag{1.9}$$

With AI

$$C_{AI} = \int_0^P h'(p)dp \tag{1.10}$$

$h'(p)$ is the rate of change of personalization and specifies how customer experience progresses with personalization.

1.6.2   Transformative Role of Blockchain in Business

Blockchain impacts businesses by increasing transparency, security, and efficiency in business operations. Blockchain technology provides real-time monitoring and eliminates intermediaries, resulting in greater trust while also lowering costs across several business processes.

Efficiency
Blockchain enhances efficiency by eliminating intermediaries, automating business processes because of smart contracts, and minimizing errors in record-keeping. For evaluating efficiency, if $C(t)$ is the cost saving over time t and $E(t)$ is the efficiency gains, then the cumulative cost savings can be given as

$$C(T) = \int_0^T E(t)dt \tag{1.11}$$

where $C(T)$ is the total cost savings.

Based on Eq. (1.11), there can be three cases:

Case 1: Constant Efficiency
If the efficiency gain $E(t)$ is constant over time, then

$$E(t) = E_0 \tag{1.12}$$

Then, the total savings $C(T)$ due to constant efficiency gain will be

$$C(T) = \int_0^T E_0 dt = E_0 T \tag{1.13}$$

This linear result shows that if efficiency remains constant, the total gains increase linearly with time.

Case 2: Linearly Increasing Efficiency
If the efficiency due to blockchain technology increases linearly over time t, then efficiency gain $E(t)$ is given as

$$E(t) = at + b \qquad (1.14)$$

where a is the rate of increase in efficiency, and b is the initial efficiency at $t = 0$.

Then, the total savings $C(T)$ due to linearly increasing efficiency gain will be

$$C(T) = \int_0^T (at + b)dt = \frac{a}{2}T^2 + bT \qquad (1.15)$$

Equation (1.15) shows that total cost savings increase quadratically for the linearly increasing efficiency.

Case 3: Exponentially Increasing Efficiency

If the efficiency due to blockchain technology increases exponentially over time t, then efficiency gain $E(t)$ is given as

$$E(t) = E_0 e^{kt} \qquad (1.16)$$

where E_0 is the initial efficiency and k is the growth rate of efficiency. Then, the total savings $C(T)$ due to exponentially increasing efficiency gain will be

$$C(T) = \int_0^T E_0 e^{kt} dt = \frac{E_0}{k} \left(e^{kT} - 1 \right) \qquad (1.17)$$

Equation (1.17) shows that if the efficiency increases exponentially, the total cost savings also increase exponentially.

Transparency

Stakeholders can access and verify the transactions on blockchain because of distributed ledger property of blockchain. This improves the transparency and helps to make faster decisions, as information asymmetry is reduced.

If $I(t)$ is the information available at time t and $T(t)$ is the transparency of the information, then the cumulative effect of transparency on decision-making can be given as

$$D(T) = \int_0^T T(t).I(t) \, dt \qquad (1.18)$$

where $D(T)$ is the improved decision-making.

There can be two cases of decision-making:

Case 1: Constant Transparency and Increasing Information

In this case, the transparency $T(t)$ remains constant and information $I(t)$ grows linearly, $T(t) = T_0$ and $I(t) = at + b$, where a is information growth and b is initial information.

Thus,

$$D(T) = \int_0^T T_0.(at+b)dt = T_0\left(\frac{a}{2}T^2 + bT\right) \tag{1.19}$$

Equation (1.19) shows that decision-making time increases quadratically with time.

Case 2: Exponentially Increasing Transparency and Information
If both transparency $T(t)$ and information $I(t)$ grow exponentially, then we can assume that:

- $T(t) = T_0 e^{kt}$, where T_0 is the initial transparency and k is the rate of transparency increase.
- $I(t) = I_0 e^{mt}$, where I_0 is the initial information level and m is the rate of information increase.

Then decision-making $D(T)$ is given as

$$D(T) = \int_0^T T_0 e^{kt}.I_0 e^{mt}.dt$$

$$= T_0 I_0 \left(\frac{e^{(k+m)T} - 1}{k + m}\right) \tag{1.20}$$

Equation (1.20) shows that with exponentially increasing transparency and information, there is cumulative effect on decision-making and it also increases exponentially.

Decision-Making
Blockchain helps in decision-making as the data stored are immutable records. If $V(t)$ represents the decision value at time t and $B(t)$ is the benefit generated due to blockchains, then

$$V(T) = \int_0^T B(t)\, dt \tag{1.21}$$

The benefit generation due to blockchain increases with time due to technological advances. Thus, if the benefit generates follows a polynomial pattern, then
$B(t) = at^2 + bt + c$, where a, b, and c are constants representing the polynomial behavior of the value generation.

$$V(T) = \int_0^T \left(at^2 + bt + c\right) dt = \frac{a}{3}T^3 + \frac{b}{2}T^2 + cT \tag{1.22}$$

Customer Experience

Blockchain helps to improve customer experience by providing more secure and transparent transactions, thereby improving trust. If $S(t)$ is the customer satisfaction at time t and $F(t)$ is the effect of blockchain in improving services, then

$$S(T) = \int_0^T F(t)\, dt \tag{1.23}$$

Blockchain reduces the transaction delay exponentially, and can be modeled as $F(t) = k.\, e^{-bt}$ where k is the initial value of function and b is the rate at which the customer experience decreases over time.

$$S(T) = \int_0^T k.e^{-bt}\, dt = \frac{k}{b}\left(1 - e^{-bT}\right) \tag{1.24}$$

1.6.3   Transformative Role of Cloud Computing in Business

Cloud computing transforms business by providing scalable, on-demand access to resources while minimizing infrastructure costs and boosting operational flexibility. It helps businesses to manage fluctuating demands effectively and improves collaborating by providing remote accessibility to data and applications.

Business Efficiency

Cloud computing helps businesses to optimize resources dynamically by adjusting the resources based on requirements. This can be modeled through cost optimization, where the aim is to minimize the total cost of ownership (TCO) as a function of computing resources.

Thus, if $C(T)$ is the total cost over time t, then it can be given by Eq. (1.25) as

$$C(T) = C_f + \int_0^T C_v(u(t))dt \tag{1.25}$$

where C_f is the fixed cost, as the subscription fees,

$C_v(u(t))$ is the variable cost which involves usage of resources at time t, and

T is the total time period.

The obvious question is to identify the resource usage by businesses at any given time t. There are three types of resources used: compute resources (e.g., CPU time), storage usage (e.g., GB stored or accessed), and network bandwidth (e.g., data transfer).

Thus, the total cost is

$$C_v(u(t)) = c_{compute}\left(u_{compute}(t)\right)$$

$$+ c_{storage}\left(u_{storage}(t)\right) + c_{bandwidth}\left(u_{bandwidth}(t)\right) \tag{1.26}$$

In Eq. (1.26)

- $c_{compute}(u_{compute}(t))$ is the overall cost of computing resources based on $u_{compute}(t)$ which represents the usage of compute resources at time t.
- $c_{storage}(u_{storage}(t))$ is the overall cost of storage based on $u_{storage}(t)$ which represents the usage of storage resources at time t.
- $c_{bandwidth}(u_{bandwidth}(t))$ is the overall cost of bandwidth used based on $u_{bandwidth}(t)$ which represents the usage of network bandwidth at time t.

$$C(T) = C_f + \int_0^T \left[c_{compute}\left(u_{compute}(t)\right) + c_{storage}\left(u_{storage}(t)\right) \right.$$

$$\left. + c_{bandwidth}\left(u_{bandwidth}(t)\right) \right] dt \tag{1.27}$$

As an example assume that company uses cloud services for a period $T = 10$ h. The total cost $C(T)$ includes:

- A fixed cost of $C_f = 600$ for a subscription fee.
- A variable cost based on the usage of compute resources, storage, and network bandwidth over time. The company has the following resource usage at any time t:

  1) Compute resource usage:
     $u_{compute}(t) = 5 + 0.2t$ *units*, with a cost per unit of compute usage, $c_{compute} = 10$
  2) Storage usage:
     $u_{storage}(t) = 10$ *GB* at a fixed rate, with a cost per GB, $c_{storage} = 2/GB$
  3) Network bandwidth usage:
     $u_{bandwidth}(t) = 1 + 0.1t$ *GB* with a cost per GB, $c_{bandwidth} = 5/GB$

Substituting the values in Eq. (1.27) and finding the total cost $C(T)$, we find that the total cost for using the cloud resources over 10 h is *1375*.

Transparency
Cloud-based platforms offer real-time monitoring of business processes and transactions, allowing transparency.

If the rate of data processing for transparency be $r(t)$ at time t which could include data logs and audit trails, the total data processed $D(T)$ over a period T can be given as

$$D(T) = \int_0^T r(t)dt \qquad (1.28)$$

The rate $r(t)$ can be expressed as a combination of different sources of data that the cloud system processes at a given time t. These sources include:

- Transaction logs at time t, $r_{trans}(t)$
- User activity logs at time t, $r_{user}(t)$
- System logs at time t, $r_{sys}(t)$

Thus, the total rate of data processing at time t can be written as:

$$r(t) = r_{trans}(t) + r_{user}(t) + r_{sys}(t) \qquad (1.29)$$

Thus,

$$D(T) = \int_0^T \left(r_{trans}(t) + r_{user}(t) + r_{sys}(t) \right) dt \qquad (1.30)$$

This gives the total amount of data processed over time, combining transaction logs, user activity logs, and system logs.

Decision-Making

Cloud computing empowers businesses to make data-driven decisions by analyzing large datasets. This can be modeled using data analytics, where historical data is analyzed to forecast future trends.

Thus, if $D(T)$ is the overall decision-making over time t, then it can be given by Eq. (1.31) as

$$D(T) = \int_0^T f(t)dt \qquad (1.31)$$

The decision-making due to cloud computing increases exponentially. Suppose $f(t) = e^{kt}$, where k is a constant.

$$D(T) = \int_0^T e^{kt}dt = \frac{1}{k}\left(e^{kT} - 1\right) \qquad (1.32)$$

Customer Experience

Cloud platforms enable businesses to enhance business experience by dynamically scaling services based on demand. This can be quantified through response time optimization, where the goal is to minimize latency as traffic increases.

If $R(t)$ be the response time at a given traffic load $l(t)$, to ensure a smooth business experience, the goal is to minimize the total response time over time

$$Minimize \ R_{total} = \int_0^T R(t)dt$$

where $R(t)$ is the response time at traffic level $l(t)$ and T is the total time period.

1.6.4 Transformative Role of Data Analytics in Business

Data analytics performs an important part in changing how businesses operate. By analyzing massive datasets, businesses can improve processes, make data-driven decisions, and improve customer satisfaction. In this part, we will study how data analytics affects the businesses with regard to business efficiency, openness, decision-making, and customer experience.

Business Efficiency
Data analytics optimizes business efficiency by uncovering bottlenecks, minimizing operating costs, and strengthening distribution of resources. Businesses can model the total time saved or efficiency improvement using the following mathematical Model for Efficiency (1.33):

$$E_{total} = E_0 + \int_0^T r(t)dt \tag{1.33}$$

If the rate of business efficiency improvement $r(t)$ increases exponentially due to data analytics, then Eq. (1.33) can be stated by Eq. (1.34).
$r(t) = e^{kt}$, where k is a constant representing the growth rate of efficiency over time,

$$E_0 = initial \ efficiency \ level$$

$$E_{total} = E_0 + \int_0^T e^{kt}dt \tag{1.34}$$

Example:
If the initial efficiency $E_0 = 100$ units and the growth rate $k = 0.05$, over 5 months, find the business efficiency gain.
Using Eq. (1.34), we get

$$E_{total} = 100 + \int_0^5 e^{0.05t}dt = 105.68 \ units$$

Thus, the business efficiency increases from 100 units to 105.68 units in 5 months.

Transparency

Data analytics helps to improve transparency by offering insights about business operations. These insights are important for making informed decisions as well as for compliance and audits.

In business, transparency can be modeled as improving with the implementation of data analytics that diminishes with time, and thus can be modeled using logarithmic function, as mentioned in Eq. (1.35)

$$T_{total} = T_0 + \int_0^T r(t)dt = T_0 + \int_0^T log(1+t)dt \tag{1.35}$$

$$T_0 = initial \ transparency \ level$$

$$log(1+t) = represents \ the \ diminshing \ rate \ transparency \ improvement \ over \ time$$

Example: If the initial transparency level is 50 (out of 100) and we want to compute the transparency level after 6 months, then using Eq. (1.35), we get

$$T_{total} = 50 + \int_0^6 log(1+6)dt = 57.62 \ units$$

The total transparency is approximately 57.62 units after 6 months.

Decision-Making

Data analytics enables data-driven decision-making by providing predictive insights and optimizing outcomes. The decision-making can be modeled by a sinusoidal function, as the effectiveness of decision-making is affected by time due to fluctuating market conditions or due to any external factors, as mentioned by Eq. (1.36)

$$D_{total} = D_0 + \int_0^T r(t)dt = D_0 + \int_0^T sin(kt)dt \tag{1.36}$$

where

$D_0 = initial \ decision \ quality$
$sin(kt) = cyclic \ nature \ of \ decision \ making$
$k = initial \ transparency \ level$

Example: Considering the initial decision quality is 200, and $k = \frac{\pi}{6}$, and we want to find the decision quality after 6 months

$$D_6 = 200 + \int_0^6 sin\left(\frac{\pi}{6}t\right)dt$$

Thus, the total decision quality after 6 months is approximately *203.82 units*.

Customer Experience

Data analytics helps businesses enhance satisfaction by analyzing customer behaviors and addressing customer requirements instantaneously. The overall customer satisfaction though quickly decays over time as well, and can thus be modeled by decaying exponential function as mentioned in Eq. (1.37)

$$C_{total} = C_0 + \int_0^T r(t)dt = C_0 + \int_0^T e^{-kt}dt \qquad (1.37)$$

where

$$C_0 = initial\ customer quality$$

$e^{-kt} = represents\ the\ rate\ of\ customer\ satisfaction, which\ slows\ down\ over\ time.$

Example: If the initial customer satisfaction $C_0 = 60$, $k = 0.2$, and we need to measure the impact in 5 months

$$C_{total} = 60 + \int_0^5 e^{-0.2t}dt = 63.16$$

Thus, the total customer satisfaction after 5 months is *63.16 units*.

1.7 Interconnectedness of ABCD Technologies

ABCD technologies—artificial intelligence, blockchain, cloud computing, and data analytics—help businesses to ease their operations and help in automated decision-making (Schmarzo, 2013; Tapscott & Tapscott, 2016), and thereby gain a competitive advantage (Hashem et al., 2014; Sun et al., 2020).

1.7.1 How ABCD Technologies Complement Each Other

To find how ABCD technologies complement each other, let's represent each of the technology using variables and do the analytical representation about their interaction.

- *Artificial intelligence (A):* AI improves data processing efficiency for business. Thus, $A = f(DS, M)$ where DS is the data size and M is the model complexity (Goodfellow et al., 2016).
- *Blockchain (B):* Blockchain improves data integrity. Mathematically, $B = g(T, S)$ where T is transaction volume and S is the security level. (Nakamoto, 2008).

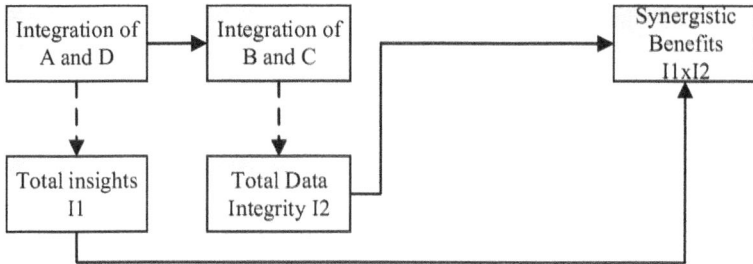

Fig. 1.2 Synergistic benefits of integrating ABCD technologies (Source: Author)

- *Cloud computing (C):* Let C depict the scalable nature of cloud computing. It can be mathematically given as $C = h(R, O)$, where R is resource availability and O is the operational demand of the resources (Mell & Grance, 2011).
- *Data analytics (D):* DA generates business insights and is represented as $DA = i(DS, Q)$ where DS is data size and Q is the quality of data (Fawcett & Provost, 2013).

1.7.2 Interconnection Between Technologies

For the sake of clarity and easy understanding, we will first integrate two technologies at a time, perform the analytical modeling, and then assess the overall efficiency of the technology. The overall efficiency of ABCD technologies is represented using symbol *E* and is called *Synergistic Benefits of Integrating ABCD technologies*. The complete outlook is shown in Fig. 1.2.

1.7.3 Integration of A and D

The integration of A and D can be represented as

$$A \times D = f(DS, M) \times i(DS, Q) \tag{1.38}$$

Equation 1.38 illustrates how A improves D's produced insights. Thus, the total insight *I*1 generated can be represented as:

$$I1 = k(A \times D) = k \times f(DS, M) \times i(DS, Q) \tag{1.39}$$

where *k* is a constant representing the synergy between A and D (Duan et al., 2019).

1.7.4   Integration of B and C

The integration of B and C is given by Eq. (1.40)

$$B \times C = g(T, S) \times h(R, O) \tag{1.40}$$

Equation 1.40 represents how blockchain ensures the integrity of data stored and processed in the cloud. The total integrity $I2$ can be represented as:

$$I2 = m(B \times C) = m \times g(T, S) \times h(R, O) \tag{1.41}$$

where m is a constant signifying the synergy between blockchain and cloud computing (Christidis & Devetsikiotis, 2016).

Based on Eqs. (1.39) and (1.41), the synergistic benefits of integrating ABCD technologies can be mathematically represented by Eq. (1.42)

$$E = \frac{I1 \times I2}{T} \tag{1.42}$$

where E represents the synergistic benefits of integrating ABCD technologies, $I1$ is the total insight generated by AI and data analytics, $I2$ represents the total integrity ensured by blockchain and cloud computing, and T is the time taken by each technology to process and implement.

Through Eq. (1.42), we can see how ABCD technologies complement each other and enhance overall business efficiency and reduce costs.

Example:

Let us consider a hypothetical case to explain synergistic benefits of integration of ABCD technologies.

A large retail chain is integrating AI, blockchain, cloud computing, and data analytics to improve its supply chain and improve consumer experience. The aim is to realize improved decision-making through predictive insights (AI + data analytics) and ensure data security and transparency in the supply chain (blockchain + cloud computing).

Step 1: Calculating I1 (Total Insights from AI and Data Analytics)

The retail chain uses AI to predict customer demand and optimize inventory management. Data analytics provides historical sales data, and AI enhances these insights by predicting future trends.

According to Duan et al. (2019), when AI is integrated, it improves the prediction accuracy by 90% by analyzing the patterns in consumer behavior. Also, Duan et al. (2019) stated that the synergy factor $k = 1.5$ is used in scenarios where AI is used to enhance data analytics process; doing so leads to 50% increase in insight generation efficiency.

Thus, $I1$ can be calculated based on Eq. (1.39) as given below:

$$I1 = k(A \ X \ D) = k \ X \ f(DS, M) \ X \ i(DS, Q) = 1.5 \ X \ (90\%) = 1.5 \ X \ 0.9 = 1.35$$

Thus, the combined use of AI and data analytics yields a 35% improvement over using only data analytics.

Step 2: Calculating I2 (Total Integrity from Blockchain and Cloud Computing)

The retail chain uses blockchain to secure supply chain transactions, ensuring data integrity. Cloud computing is used to store and process this data efficiently.

According to Christidis and Devetsikiotis (2016), by integrating blockchain, the data security improves by 99.9% for all transactions. Christidis and Devetsikiotis (2016) also mentioned that synergy factor $m = 1.2$ is observed where blockchain enhances the reliability and security of cloud-based operations by 20%.

Thus, $I2$ can be calculated based on Eq. (1.41)

$$I2 = m(B \ X \ C) = m \ X \ g(T, S) \ X \ h(R, O) = 1.2 \ X \ (99.9\%) = 1.2 \ X \ 0.999 = 1.1988$$

The integration of blockchain and cloud computing improves data integrity by about 19.88%.

Step 3: Calculating T (Time Taken to Process and Implement Technologies)

Manyika et al.(2011) mention that it takes several hours ($\approx$5 h) to generate predictive insights using AI and data analytics, and Deloitte (2016) suggests that blockchain transactions, while secure, can take anywhere from a few minutes to several hours to be validated ($\approx$3 h).

Thus, total time T taken by all the technologies is

$$T = 5 + 3 = 8 \ h$$

Step 4: Calculating the Synergistic Benefits E
Based on Eq. (1.42), we get

$$E = \frac{I1 \ x \ I2}{T} = \frac{1.35 \ X \ 1.1988}{8} = \frac{1.61838}{8} \approx 0.2023$$

The overall synergistic benefit of integrating ABCD technologies is approximately 20.23% efficiency gain relative to the total time taken. This value suggests that the integration of these ABCD technologies provides a significant improvement in decision-making, security, and overall process efficiency.

1.7.5 Cost Efficiency and Resource Optimization

Another benefit of integrating ABCD technology for businesses is that it leads to greater cost savings than the sum when they are used individually. This concept is called as synergistic savings.

If we define the cost function of assimilating ABCD technology as $C(x)$, and synergistic savings as $S(x)$, then the cost function can be represented as:

$$C(x) = C_0 - S(x)$$

where C_0 is the initial cost without synergy and $C_0 = A + B + C + D$.

If α is the synergy factor that defines cost efficiency and resource optimization, then the cost function $C(x)$ can be defined as:

$$C(x) = [A + B + C + D] - \alpha.S(x)$$

1.7.6   Real-Time Analytics and Decision-Making Speed

If we quantify the impact of integrating ABCD technologies on decision-making, then the decision-making speed can be mathematically given as

$$D_{speed\ (initial)} = \frac{1}{T_{process\ (initial)}}$$

where $T_{process\ (initial)}$ is the total processing time.

Exercise

Exercise 1: To understand the fundamental definitions and key concepts of ABCD technologies

Business Scenario

GlobalMart is a retail company located in numerous nations, selling market goods both online and through shops. The company tries to simplify processes, increase customer satisfaction, and boost decision-making by adopting new technologies. GlobalMart uses AI-powered chatbots to handle customer queries online. These chatbots understand customer problems, and react in real time, lowering the need for human intervention. Additionally, for online, AI helps predict customer demand through analyzing shopping behavior as well as preferences, allowing the GlobalMart to improve its inventory.

GlobalMart uses blockchain to improve transparency in its supply chain. Each activity, from purchase to distribution, can be tracked on a blockchain, ensuring every participant (suppliers, stores, wholesalers) has real-time access to data. This transparency allows for monitoring the origin of goods, ensuring that goods are identified accurately and reducing frauds or disruptions in delivery.

GlobalMart uses cloud computing to grow its e-commerce platform during peak shopping seasons. The cloud technology helps GlobalMart to raise its server capacity quickly to handle a spike in web traffic. This ensures smooth shopping experience without interruptions, and GlobalMart only pays for the additional resources it uses during these periods.

GlobalMart uses data analytics to understand customer behavior better. By examining purchase history and preferences, GlobalMart can make data-driven choices about product sales and discounts. Predictive analytics models help predict future sales trends, while prescriptive analytics suggest the ideal stock levels to keep to avoid overstocking or understocking during different seasons.

Tasks and deliverables: You are required to write a report summarizing the use of ABCD technologies by GlobalMart.

Exercise 2: Business Impact Analysis

There are four business scenarios given below and you are required to analyze the impact of ABCD technologies on business operations.

Business Scenario 1:
Industry: E-commerce
Company: Flipkart

Flipkart, one of India's largest e-commerce platforms, uses AI to enhance customer experiences. AI powers product recommendations, personalized search results, and voice recognition features. Flipkart's AI-driven chatbots interact with customers in multiple languages and thus answer queries in almost all major Indian languages.

Business Scenario 2:
Industry: Financial services
Company: Yes Bank

Yes Bank adopted blockchain technology to improve its financing operations. Blockchain helps digitize processes, ensuring secure, transparent, and real-time data sharing. Also using smart contracts, Yes Bank automates and enforces the terms of agreement between parties.

Business Scenario 3:
Industry: Media and entertainment
Company: Hotstar (now Disney+ Hotstar)

Hotstar, a popular Indian streaming service, uses cloud computing to deliver video content to millions of users, even during high-traffic events like the Indian

Premier League (IPL). The scalability of cloud infrastructure allows Hotstar to handle massive user traffic spikes, ensuring uninterrupted service during live events.

Business Scenario 4:
Industry: Retail
Company: Reliance Retail

Reliance Retail, India's largest retail chain, uses data analytics to understand customer buying patterns, predict demand, and optimize inventory. By analyzing data from millions of transactions, Reliance Retail tailors product offerings to suit different regions and customer preferences. Data analytics also helps improve supply chain management by predicting stock shortages and optimizing warehouse management.

Task and deliverables: Discuss how ABCD technology has transformed the industries as mentioned in the four business scenarios above.

Exercise 3: Interconnectedness of Technologies

A retailer needs to optimize its supply chain as it faces challenges such as demand forecasting, data integrity, resource allocation in the cloud, and securing transactions across its supply chain. To solve these problems, the retailer decides to integrate artificial intelligence, blockchain, cloud computing, and data analytics.

The retailer uses AI to improve the demand forecasting and data analytics to refine the predictions. It was observed that AI model improves the demand forecasting by 85% and data analytics refined the predictions by 90%.

The retailer further uses blockchain to secure all its transactions and cloud computing to process the transactions securely. The outcomes are that blockchain improves the transactions by 99.8% and 72% of data is secured by cloud computing.

It is also observed that the synergy factor for integrating AI and data analytics is 1.5, and the synergy factor for integrating blockchain and cloud computing is 1.2.

The total time to process and implement both technologies is 4 h.

Evaluate the overall efficiency of implementing the ABCD technologies.

Hint:

$$I1 = k(A \times D) = 1.5 \times 0.85 \times 0.9 = 1.1475$$

$$I2 = m(B \times C) = 1.2 \times 0.998 \times 0.72 = 0.8628$$

$$E = \frac{I1 \times I2}{T} = \frac{1.1475 \times 0.8628}{4} = 0.247$$

Thus overall efficiency for the retailer increases by 24.7% after implementing ABCD technologies.

Exercise 4: Case Study Analysis

Assume an online retailer uses cloud services for improving business efficiency. The total cost $C(T)$ includes:

- A fixed subscription fee: $C_f = 600$
- A variable cost based on compute, storage, and network usage, with the following usage patterns:

    - *Compute resource usage*:
        $u_{compute}(t) = 8 + 0.3t$ *units*, with a cost per unit of compute usage, $c_{compute} = 15$
    - *Storage usage*:
        $u_{storage}(t) = 20$ *GB* at a fixed rate, with a cost per GB, $c_{storage} = 3/GB$
    - *Network bandwidth usage*:
        $u_{bandwidth}(t) = 2 + 0.2t$ *GB* with a cost per GB, $c_{bandwidth} = 10/GB$

The company also uses cloud-based platforms to track transaction logs, user behavior, and system activities. The logs grow over time with the following rates:

- *Transaction logs at time t*, $r_{trans}(t) = 5 + 0.2t$
- *User activity logs at time t*, $r_{user}(t) = 3$
- *System logs at time t*, $r_{sys}(t) = 2 + 0.1t$

The company has also employed cloud-based data analytics to forecast future sales trends. The rate of decision-making grows exponentially with $k = 0.05$ by using cloud-based analytics.

To ensure customer experience especially during peak hours, online retailer has modeled the response time using cloud-based platform to be $R(t) = 1 + 0.1t$.

The company wants to conduct a detailed analysis of how the implementation of cloud computing has improved business outcomes. (For simplicity, the company wants to test the results for 10 h.)

Results
In this scenario, cloud computing enhances the business's operational efficiency, transparency, decision-making, and customer experience:

- *Business efficiency*: The total cloud service cost for 10 h is *2925*, reflecting resource usage (compute, storage, and network bandwidth).
- *Transparency*: The cloud platform processes *115 units of data*, providing real-time insights into business operations.
- *Decision-making*: Cloud-based analytics improves decision-making by *12.97 ≈ 13 times* over 10 h.
- *Customer experience*: The total response time during peak times is *15 times*.

References

Ahmed, M., Mahmood, A., & Hu, J. (2015). A survey of network anomaly detection techniques. *Journal of Network and Computer Applications, 60*, 19–31. https://doi.org/10.1016/j.jnca.2015.11.016

Chen, C., Fu, H., Zheng, Y., Tao, F., & Liu, Y. (2023). The advance of digital twin for predictive maintenance: The role and function of machine learning. *Journal of Manufacturing Systems, 71*, 581–594. https://doi.org/10.1016/j.jmsy.2023.10.010

Christidis, K., & Devetsikiotis, M. (2016). Blockchains and smart contracts for the internet of things. *IEEE Access, 4*, 2292–2303. IEEE Access. https://doi.org/10.1109/ACCESS.2016.2566339

Deloitte. (2016). *Blockchain—Enigma Paradox Opportunity | Deloitte Switzerland | Innovation.* Deloitte. https://www2.deloitte.com/ch/en/pages/innovation/articles/blockchain.html

Duan, Y., Edwards, J., & Dwivedi, Y. (2019). Artificial intelligence for decision making in the era of Big Data – evolution, challenges and research agenda. *International Journal of Information Management, 48*, 63–71. https://doi.org/10.1016/j.ijinfomgt.2019.01.021

Fawcett, T., & Provost, F. (2013). *Data science for business.*

Goodfellow, I., Bengio, Y., & Courville, A. (2016). *Deep learning.* MIT Press.

Hashem, I., Yaqoob, I., Anuar, N., Mokhtar, S., Gani, A., & Khan, S. (2014). The rise of "Big Data" on cloud computing: Review and open research issues. *Information Systems, 47*, 98–115. https://doi.org/10.1016/j.is.2014.07.006

Manyika, J., Chui, M., Brown, B., Bughin, J., Dobbs, R., Roxburgh, C., & Byers, A. (2011). *Big data: The Next frontier for innovation, competition, and productivity.*

Mell, P. M., & Grance, T. (2011). *SP 800-145. The NIST Definition of Cloud Computing* [Technical Report]. National Institute of Standards & Technology.

Mitchell, T. M. (2013). *Machine learning* (Nachdr.). McGraw-Hill.

Nakamoto, S. (2008). *Bitcoin: A peer-to-peer electronic cash system* (SSRN Scholarly Paper 3440802). https://doi.org/10.2139/ssrn.3440802

Necula, S.-C. (2023). Exploring the impact of time spent reading product information on e-commerce websites: A machine learning approach to analyze consumer behavior. *Behavioral Sciences, 13*(6), 439. https://doi.org/10.3390/bs13060439

Richey, R. G., Jr., Chowdhury, S., Davis-Sramek, B., Giannakis, M., & Dwivedi, Y. K. (2023). Artificial intelligence in logistics and supply chain management: A primer and roadmap for research. *Journal of Business Logistics, 44*(4), 532–549. https://doi.org/10.1111/jbl.12364

Schmarzo, B. (2013). *Big data: Understanding how data powers big business.* https://www.semanticscholar.org/paper/Big-Data%3A-Understanding-How-Data-Powers-Big-Schmarzo/50e47757ad821b74efc12592de4fa7de27bdd192

Soori, M., Arezoo, B., & Dastres, R. (2023). Artificial intelligence, machine learning and deep learning in advanced robotics, a review. *Cognitive Robotics, 3*, 54–70. https://doi.org/10.1016/j.cogr.2023.04.001

SphereGen. (2020). *Blockchain technology basics.* SphereGen. https://www.spheregen.com/blockchain-technology-basics/

Sun, L., Jiang, X., Ren, H., & Guo, Y. (2020). Edge-cloud computing and artificial intelligence in internet of medical things: Architecture, technology and application. *IEEE Access, 1.* https://doi.org/10.1109/ACCESS.2020.2997831

Tapscott, D., & Tapscott, A. (2016). *Blockchain revolution: How the technology behind bitcoin is changing money, business, and the world.* Penguin Publishing Group.

Yixuan, Z. (2024). Utilizing machine learning algorithms for consumer behaviour analysis. *Applied and Computational Engineering, 49*, 213–219. https://doi.org/10.54254/2755-2721/49/20241186

Chapter 2
Understanding Artificial Intelligence

Abstract This chapter examines how artificial intelligence (AI) and machine learning (ML) may help businesses evolve. It offers a fundamental overview of AI, including its history, types, and algorithms. The chapter analyzes the economic implications of AI adoption, emphasizing advantages such as revenue growth, cost savings, efficiency improvements, and risk reduction, which are depicted using mathematical models. Several AI applications in business processes are discussed, including process automation, decision-making, and customer experience adaptation. AI-powered automation, predictive analytics, and supply chain optimization are among the key themes highlighted, as well as potential futures. Ethical issues for AI adoption are also discussed, including a job displacement, privacy, bias, and transparency. The chapter ends by discussing legal frameworks such as GDPR and HIPAA, highlighting the need for compliance in ensuring responsible AI usage in businesses such as banking, healthcare, and human resources.

Keywords Artificial intelligence (AI) · Machine learning (ML) · Economic impact of AI · AI trends · Ethical AI · Regulatory frameworks · Revenue growth · Cost reduction · Pricing models

2.1 Introduction

The chapter delves further into AI and machine learning, as well as its implications for business. The chapter's goal is to give readers with both basic information and practical insights into AI's role in corporate transformation. The chapter opens with an fundamentals of AI and ML, including history, types, and basic algorithms. The second section discusses the economic implications of AI adoption, demonstrating how AI generates revenue growth, cost savings, efficiency benefits, risk reduction, and return on investment (ROI) for all three kinds of ML using hypothetical scenarios. The chapter goes on to look at various AI applications for optimizing business operations, particularly in AI in Business Process. Finally, in the last part, the chapter discusses future trends and ethical considerations for AI, providing insights into the responsible and strategic use of AI in business.

2.2   Fundamentals of AI and ML

AI and ML are two transformational technologies that are altering the way we do business. The section begins with a history of artificial intelligence, charting its progression from mythical ideas to the complex systems used today. The section delves more into the many forms of AI, ranging from narrow AI, which is intended to accomplish certain tasks, to general AI, which seeks to reproduce human-like cognitive abilities. Within AI, the three forms of narrow AI—ML, neural networks (NN), and natural language processing (NLP)—are thoroughly addressed.

2.2.1   History of AI

The history of artificial intelligence is a rich complex journey spanning many centuries, beginning with early philosophical research regarding the nature of thoughts and intellect.

Early Foundations (1940s–1950s)
The early foundations of AI began when Alan Turing published a research paper *Computing Machinery and Intelligence* in 1950 (Turing, 1950). In the paper, Turing introduced the concept of machines performing tasks that require human intelligence and named it *Turing Test*. At the same time, John von Neumann laid the foundation of computer architecture capable of performing the logical operations (Al-Hashimi, 2023).

In 1955, Allen Newell and Herbert Simon proposed the early AI programs that could solve the mathematical problems simulating the human brain process. They called the program *Logic Theorist* (Gugerty, 2006).

In 1956, John McCarthy, Marvin Minsky, Nathaniel Rochester, and Claude Shannon organized conference at Dartmouth College, where the term *artificial intelligence* was coined and was proposed to be part of the academic curriculum (Dick, 2019).

The 1960s saw the growth of AI with programs that simulate human behavior. Some of the programs developed are *Symbolic AI, ELIZA*, and *SHRDLU* (Toews, 2019). This was the time when first robotics and machine learning algorithms were also developed, laying the foundation of future AI developments.

The 1960s witnessed the early optimism surrounding AI, motivated by the expectation that human-level artificial intelligence may be realized in the near future. Researchers like Marvin Minsky and John McCarthy, who were among the pioneers of AI, played crucial roles at that time. They anticipated that AI could imitate human intellect within a few decades (Jiang et al., 2022).

The 1970s witnessed considerable developments in expert systems, which were AI meant to imitate human competence in specific domains. One well-known example is *MYCIN*, a rule-based system built for medical diagnostics (Yoon &

Adya, 2003). These systems exhibited AI's capacity to solve practical, real-world challenges, notably in decision-making domains.

Amid early enthusiasm, by the late 1970s, it became evident that AI technology had limitations. AI systems had restricted capacity because of limited processing power, and also failed to scale up without access to massive datasets. These issues, along with overpromising and under delivering, led to a disappointment called as the AI Winter (Toosi et al., 2021). During this period, funding for AI research was substantially reduced, and development stalled considerably. Many in the scientific community became doubtful about AI's capacity to acquire human-like intelligence in the near future.

In the 1980s, AI saw a revival, partly owing to the discovery of neural networks. The creation of the backpropagation method by Geoffrey Hinton, David Rumelhart, and others allowed for successful training of neural networks, which permitted to handle challenging tasks (Werbos, 1988). Also, this time saw a move from the previous rule-based expert systems to learning-based systems, where AI models could learn patterns from data instead of depending on predefined rules. Neural networks become key to this new method. The success of neural networks in handling non-linear problems, such as pattern recognition, renewed interest and investment in AI, signaling the end of the AI Winter.

In the early 2000s, an exponential rise of big data and the emergence of powerful computer infrastructure prepared the path for improvements in AI. With access to enormous datasets and upgraded technology (like GPUs), AI researchers could train more complicated models, notably neural networks. This decade witnessed the emergence of deep learning, a subset of AI that focuses on training huge, multi-layered neural networks to identify trends in data. Researchers like Geoffrey Hinton, Yann LeCun, and Yoshua Bengio were pioneers in this development. Deep learning proved particularly successful in applications such as image identification, audio processing, and natural language understanding (Emmert-Streib et al., 2020).

By the 2010s, AI has progressed beyond research laboratories into daily use. Speech recognition became prevalent with the development of virtual assistants like Siri (Apple) and Google Assistant (Rafiq, 2023). AI also finds significant usage in computer vision, enabling applications like face recognition and autonomous vehicles (Garikapati & Shetiya, 2024). AI started to drive recommendation engines, with businesses like Netflix (Medium, 2023) and Amazon (Haleem et al., 2022) applying it to propose movies, products, and services based on customer interests and activity.

In 2016, AlphaGo, an AI built by Google DeepMind, beat the world champion in the complicated board game of Go (Borowiec, 2016). This was a tremendous advance, displaying the capability of deep neural networks paired with reinforcement learning. It proved AI's capacity to solve strategic and complex issues that were previously believed out of reach for AI.

By the 2020s, as AI was more used in daily life, concerns regarding its ethical usage have increased (Parsons, 2020). Issues such as biases in AI systems, privacy issues, and the possibility for job displacement have spurred worldwide conversations regarding the ethical development and use of AI technology. There is a rising need for AI regulatory frameworks to guarantee that AI is created in a manner that is fair, transparent, and responsible (*which is also discussed in Sect. 2.5.3 of the chapter*). Policymakers, academics, and businesses are actively considering how to make ethical use of AI while supporting innovation. As AI continues to advance, setting guidelines for ethical AI has become an emphasis area.

2.2.2 Basic Concept of AI and ML

We already know that AI enables a machine to perform tasks that require human intelligence. The way machine does that is to learn from the data and then make decisions to achieve specific goals. The section of AI that makes machine learn from the data and perform the tasks is called machine learning or ML. There are three categories of AI:

1. *Narrow AI*: AI systems that are designed for specific tasks by learning from the data.
2. *General AI*: AI systems that can perform the intellectual tasks that human can do.
3. *Superintelligence AI*: AI systems that surpass human intelligence across all fields.

General AI (GAI) and superintelligence AI (SAI) do not exist and still remain theoretical concepts to date.

ML is a type of narrow AI wherein the systems learn from the data and improve over time without even programmed.

There are four types of ML (as is already discussed in Chap. 1):

1. Descriptive ML
2. Diagnostic ML
3. Predictive ML
4. Prescriptive ML

Though we study in detail about each type of ML in Chap. 5, here we are going to understand the types of ML with basic examples.

2.2.2.1 Brief Description About Each Type ML

Descriptive ML
Descriptive ML is used to summarize the data and based on which businesses understand trends and patterns. The common type of descriptive ML is given below:

- *Data aggregation:* Data aggregation means summarizing large datasets to understand the patterns. For example, retail stores use data aggregation to see the sales across multiple stores and then calculate the total revenue.
- *Data visualization:* Data visualization represents the data in pictorial format (such as bar charts, pie charts, histograms, or line charts) and then understand the trends

or patterns. For example, the company generates the pie chart to see the portion sales of particular items at all of its stores.

- *Reporting:* Reporting the structured summary of the historical data, which is also called dashboards. A monthly marketing report or the monthly employee attendance report is an example of reporting.
- Summary Statistics is the most common type of descriptive analytics analytics. Descriptive analytics used and calculates the basic statistical measures such as mean (average), median, mode, variance, and standard deviation, which help summarize the distribution and central tendencies in the data, for example, calculating the average sales or finding the standard deviations in the weights of the products to find product consistency.

Diagnostic ML

The diagnostic ML helps to understand the reasons behind the past events by analyzing the trends, patterns, or correlations. The three main techniques for diagnostic ML are:

- *Correlation analysis:* Correlation analysis helps to understand the relationship between two or more variables and determine if they are correlated or not. For example, we can find the correlation between social media reviews and online sales.
- *Time series analysis:* Time-series analysis involves analyzing the data collected over a longer time period to identify the trends, seasonality, or cycles. For example, we can use the time-series analysis to understand the sale of the particular product over a period of time and then identify on which months the sale is high.
- *Hypotheses testing:* Hypotheses testing is used to make statistical inferences about population based on the sample data. We can use hypotheses testing to test whether the particular marketing campaign helps to increase sales or not.

Predictive ML

Predictive ML uses the historical data and uses the ML to forecast the future. There are two types of predictive ML that are commonly used by businesses: *supervised* and *unsupervised* learning.

Supervised learning

In supervised learning, the model is built on labeled data, where the input data and output label are given. The objective is for the model to gain insights into the relation between inputs and outputs to make predictions on new, unknown data.

The types of supervised predictive analytics are:

(1) Classification: Classification predicts binary results by giving data points to one of several classes, for example, to classify the email as spam or not spam, or the transaction as fraud or not fraud. The algorithms are Decision Trees, Logistic Regression, Support Vector Machines (SVM), and Random Forest.

(2) Regression: Regression predicts continuous numerical results determined by input variables. It describes the association between dependent and

independent variables, for example, to predict the house price based on location and the number of bedrooms, or sales forecast based on advertising and market trends. The algorithms are Simple Linear Regression and Multiple Linear Regression.

(3) Time-series forecasting: Time-series forecasting examines datasets gathered over time to predict future values based on trends, seasonality, and cycles. A retailer uses time-series forecasting to predict future demand for a product based on prior sales data. The algorithms are ARIMA model (Auto-Regressive Integrated Moving Average) and VAR model.

Unsupervised learning

In unsupervised learning, the model is trained on data without labels. The aim is to find patterns, structures, or relationships inside the data. Although unsupervised learning is more frequently associated with descriptive and diagnostic analytics, it can also be used in predictive analytics to group data and make predictions based on trends.

The types of unsupervised predictive analytics are:

(1) Clustering: Clustering is used in predictive analytics to group data points into clusters, allowing businesses to predict outcomes based on group characteristics. A company uses clustering to group customers into segments and predict which group is more likely to respond to a new marketing campaign. The algorithms are K-Means Clustering and Hierarchical Clustering.

(2) Association rule mining: Association rule mining discovers correlations or trends between variables within huge datasets. Examples include predicting which products are likely to be purchased together based on transaction history or giving recommendations to customers based on products which are bought together. The algorithms are Apriori Algorithm, Eclat Algorithm, and FP-Growth (Frequent Pattern Growth).

Prescriptive ML

Prescriptive ML uses data, algorithms, and predictive models for recommending specific measures for improved decision-making. It goes beyond forecasting outcomes to provide actionable insights into what needs to be done to achieve the intended outcome. Prescriptive machine learning assists businesses in areas such as supply chain optimization, targeted marketing, and financial planning by simulating multiple situations, allowing them to assess the optimal action based on desired outcomes.

2.3 Economic Implications of AI Adoption

AI adoption is economically transforming the businesses in three ways: (a) revenue growth, (b) reducing costs, (c) efficiency gains, and (d) risk reduction. In this section, we will cover all of the abovementioned benefits of AI with examples.

2.3.1   *Revenue Growth with AI*

AI helps businesses to increase the revenue through customized suggestions and dynamic pricing among others (Gatera, 2024). If $R(t)$ is the revenue at time t, then the rate of revenue can be defined as

$$\frac{dR(t)}{dt} = \alpha.R(t) \tag{2.1}$$

In Eq. (2.1) α is the growth rate constant which indicates revenue growth due to AI.

Eq. (2.1) assumes that revenue will continue indefinitely; however, market may decline due to saturation or competition. Thus, the limiting factor K is introduced. As the revenue reaches K, the growth slows down, and the rate of revenue can be given by Eq. (2.2):

$$\frac{dR(t)}{dt} = \alpha.R(t)\left(1 - \frac{R(t)}{K}\right) \tag{2.2}$$

In Eq. (2.2), $1 - \frac{R(t)}{K}$ represents the fraction of the market that has not yet been captured. When $R(t)$ is small, $1 - \frac{R(t)}{K}$ is close to 1, which means that there is growth potential, and as $R(t)$ approaches K, the growth potential is less.

The final equation of revenue $R(t)$ can be obtained by integrating Eq. (2.2), and is as given in Eq. (2.3)

$$R(t) = \frac{K}{1 + \left(\frac{K - R_0}{R_0}\right)e^{-\alpha t}} \tag{2.3}$$

To understand the working of Eq. (2.3), suppose a company has an initial revenue $R_0 = 10,000$. The company operates in a market with limiting factor $K = 100,000$. The growth rate α is 0.1 per year. We want to determine the revenue $R(t)$ at any time t and specifically calculate $R(t)$ after 5 years.

If we substitute the given data in Eq. (2.3), we get

$$R(5) = \frac{100,000}{1 + \left(\frac{100,000 - 10,000}{10,000}\right)e^{-0.1*5}} = 15,480.94$$

Thus, after 5 years, the revenue of the company will be 15,480.94, and will continue till the limiting factor, $K = 100,000$.

As an example, businesses like *Amazon* and *Netflix* experienced rapid growth initially; however, due to increased competition and market saturation, their growth rates moderated despite continued revenue increases.

2.3.2   *Reducing Costs with AI*

The cost reduction due to the use of AI can be modeled using optimization problem, wherein we are required to minimize the cost subject to constraints (Islam et al., 2020). The best method to solve the optimization problem is through Lagrange multiplier (Vadlamani et al., 2020).

If total cost, $C(L, A)$, depends on

- Labor cost (L), and
- AI investment (A)

then *objective function* is given by Eq. (2.4)

$$C(L, A) = C_0 - \gamma_1 L^2 - \gamma_2 A^2 \tag{2.4}$$

The equation shows that cost $C(L, A)$ decreases as labor L is reduced and as AI investment A increases. γ_1 and γ_2 are constants representing the effects of labor and AI on cost reduction, respectively.

Constraint:

The constraints are the total cost of labor (L) and AI (A), which should not exceed budget, B. Thus,

$$L + A = B \rightarrow B - L - A \tag{2.5}$$

Lagrange Multiplier Approach:

Now, the we need to set the Lagrange multiplier approach, which combines total cost and constraints using the new variable λ.

$$L(L, A, \lambda) = C(L, A) + \lambda(B - L - A) \tag{2.6}$$

Differentiating the equation w.r.t L, A, λ, we get Eqs. (2.7), (2.8), and (2.9), respectively

$$\frac{\partial L}{\partial L} = -2\gamma_1 L - \lambda = 0 \rightarrow \lambda = -2\gamma_1 L \tag{2.7}$$

$$\frac{\partial L}{\partial A} = -2\gamma_2 A - \lambda = 0 \rightarrow \lambda = -2\gamma_2 A \tag{2.8}$$

$$\frac{\partial L}{\partial \lambda} = B - L - A = 0 \rightarrow L + A = B \tag{2.9}$$

Equating Eqs. (2.7) and (2.8)

$$-2\gamma_1 L = -2\gamma_2 A$$

$$L = \frac{\gamma_2}{\gamma_1} A \tag{2.10}$$

Also, substituting Eq. (2.10) into constraint Eq. (2.9), we get

$$L + A = B \rightarrow \frac{\gamma_2}{\gamma_1} A + A = B$$

$$A = \frac{B\gamma_1}{(\gamma_1 + \gamma_2)} \tag{2.11}$$

Thus, the equation of L is

$$L = \frac{B\gamma_2}{(\gamma_1 + \gamma_2)} \tag{2.12}$$

Example, if $B = 100$,

$\gamma_1 = 2$ (*Labor cost coefficient*)
$\gamma_2 = 3$ (*AI cost coefficient*)

Cost without AI:
As there is no AI cost involved, the constraint is

$$L = B$$

and the cost function includes labor cost only

$$C(L, 0) = C_0 \quad \gamma_1 L^2 = C_0 \quad \gamma_1 B^2$$

Thus, cost without AI is

$$C(L, 0) = 1000 - 2.(100)^2 = -19{,}000$$

Cost with AI:

$$A = \frac{B\gamma_1}{(\gamma_1 + \gamma_2)} = 100$$

$$L = \frac{\gamma_2}{\gamma_1} A = 60$$

Total cost with AI is

$$C(L,A) = 1000 - 2(60)^2 - 3(40)^2 = -11,000$$

Thus, cost reduces from 19,000 to 11,000 with AI.

2.3.3   Efficiency Gains with AI

The efficiency gains with AI for businesses can be evaluated using the Cobb–Douglas production function. The model represents the relationship between inputs (such as capital, labor, and AI) and finds the efficiency gains for businesses.

Mathematically, the Cobb–Douglas production function can be given in Eq. (2.13)

$$E(K,L,A) = A_0.K^\alpha.L^{1-\alpha} \tag{2.13}$$

where

$K = amount\ of\ capital\ invested$
$L = Labor\ involved$
$A = Investment\ in\ AI$
$A_0 = Base\ efficieny\ constant\ without\ AI$
$K^\alpha = if\ capital\ K\ increases,\ efficiency\ also\ increases\ to\ the\ power\ \alpha$
$L^{1-\alpha} = if\ labor\ increases,\ efficiency\ also\ increases\ to\ the\ power\ 1 - \alpha$

Efficiency gain without AI:
If without AI, $A_0 = 10$, $K = 100$, and $l = 50$.
   $\alpha = 0.4$ (means 40% efficiency comes from capital and 60% from labor)

$$E(K,L,A) = 10.100^{0.4}.50^{1-0.4} \approx 882.31$$

Thus, without AI the efficiency gain is approximately, 882.31.

Efficiency gain with AI:
With AI investments, the overall efficiency increase is reflected by an increase in base efficiency constant.

Let us assume that AI boosts the base efficiency constant $A_0 = 10$ to $A_0' = 15$
Thus,

$$E'(K,L,A) = 15.100^{0.4}.50^{1-0.4} \approx 1323.47$$

Overall, efficiency gain

$$\Delta E = 1323.47 - 882.31 = 441.16\ units\ of\ efficiency\ gain.$$

2.3.4 Risk Reduction with AI

The risk reduction can be calculated using predictive analytics and proactive risk management. We will be using stochastic differential equation (SDE) to describe how AI impacts risk reduction. Equation (2.14) explains the equation

$$dR(t) = -\lambda R(t)dt + \sigma R(t)dW_t \qquad (2.14)$$

In Eq. (2.14),

$dR(t) =$ *change of risk over time*
$\lambda =$ *rate of risk reduction over time*
$\sigma =$ *uncertainity is risk reduction (volatility)*
$dW_t =$ *Wiener process that models random motion over time in stochastic process*

Risk Reduction without AI:
Based on Eq. (2.14), the risk reduction without AI is given as:

$$dR(t) = \sigma R(t)dW_t \qquad (2.15)$$

The first part from Eq. (2.14) is not considered because there is no risk management.

Example:
Without AI: Suppose risk starts at 100 units. Over time, the risk will fluctuate due to market conditions. At time $t = 1$, risk might increase to 105 or decrease to 95, depending on the Wiener process, with no systematic reduction.

With AI: Starting at 100 units, AI systematically reduces risk. At $t = 1$, the systematic reduction of 5% brings risk down to 95 units (because $100 - (0.05 \times 100) = 95$). While the stochastic term might add some fluctuation, the overall trend will be downward. At $t = 2$, risk might reduce further to around 90 units, modulated by random fluctuations.

2.4 AI in Business Process

AI has a disruptive impact on business operations by *automating processes, improving decision-making, streamlining supply chains, increasing customer satisfaction,* and *decreasing expenses*. In this section, we examine particular AI applications in business processes using mathematical models and examples.

2.4.1   AI in Process Automation

AI helps to automate the repetitive tasks through robotic process automation (RPA). RPA leads to increased efficiency and reduces the operational costs to do the repetitive tasks.

If N is the number of tasks (which also include repetitive tasks) and T is the time required to complete these tasks manually, the efficiency to complete all the tasks can be given by Eq. (2.16)

$$E_{manual} = \frac{N}{T} \tag{2.16}$$

With the introduction of AI, X% of the tasks (which are repetitive) gets reduced and the overall efficiency is as stated in Eq. (2.17)

$$E_{AI} = \frac{N}{T_{AI}} \tag{2.17}$$

To see how AI impacts efficiency, we take the derivative of Eq. (2.17)

$$\frac{dE_{AI}}{dT_{AI}} = -\frac{N}{T_{AI}^2} \tag{2.18}$$

Equation (2.18) shows that as T_{AI} decreases, efficiency increases.

Example:
Assume that the business is using RPA to minimize the time required to complete the business orders. The business requires to process 1000 orders in 10 h every day. After the introduction of AI, it is observed that 30% of the tasks are repetitive, and thus the time required to process these orders can be reduced. Find the new efficiency of processing orders and the rate of change of efficiency change.

Using Eq. (2.16), we have

$E_{manual} = \frac{1000}{10} = 100$ orders per hour

With the introduction of AI, 30% of the tasks (which are repetitive) get reduced and the overall efficiency can be taken from Eq. (2.17)

$$T_{AI} = 10 \ X \ (1 - 0.30) = 7 \ h$$

$E_{AI} = \frac{1000}{7} \approx 142.86$ orders per hour

Rate of change of efficiency $\frac{dE_{AI}}{dT_{AI}} = -\frac{1000}{7^2} = -20.41$ orders per hour^2

The negative sign shows that efficiency increases as processing time decreases.

2.4.2   AI to Improve Decision-Making

AI uses predictive analytics to forecast future events, which helps businesses to make informed decisions. Assume that the business uses predictive model using simple linear regression model to predict sales $S(t)$. The sales depends on historical data for marketing spend (M) and seasonal factors $\theta(t)$.

$$S(t) = \alpha + \beta_1 M + \beta_2 \theta(t) \tag{2.19}$$

where α is intercept and β_1, β_2 are regression coefficients.

The rate of change of sales with respect to time is given as

$$\frac{dS(t)}{dt} = \beta_2 \frac{d\theta(t)}{dt} \tag{2.20}$$

Equation (2.20) shows how seasonal variations affect sales over time.

The total sales over time (from $t = 0$ to $t = T$) are given by Eq. (2.21)

$$S_{total} = \int_0^T (\alpha + \beta_1 M + \beta_2 \theta(t)).dt \tag{2.21}$$

If $\theta(t) = \sin(t)$ [seasonal factor], then total sales can be given by Eq. (2.22)

$$S_{total} = \alpha T + \beta_1 MT + \beta_2 (1 - \cos(T)) \tag{2.22}$$

Example:
A company wants to forecast sales based on the marketing spend M and a seasonal factor $\theta(t) = \sin(t)$. The sales prediction model is

$$S(t) = 500 + 10M + 100 \sin(t)$$

Find the total sales over a period of 6 months $T = 6$ if marketing spend $M = 200$.
Step 1: Define the sales function.

$$S(t) = 500 + 10M + 100 \sin(t)$$

Substitute $M = 200$ into the sales function:

$$S(t) = 500 + 10(200) + 100 \sin(t) = 2500 + 100 \sin(t)$$

Step 2: Integrate the sales function over 6 months. To find the total sales over 6 months, using Eq. (2.21), we get

$$S_{total} = \int_0^T (\alpha + \beta_1 M + \beta_2 \theta(t)).dt = \int_0^6 (2500 + 100 \sin(t)).dt = 15{,}003.98$$

Thus, the total predicted sales over 6 months are approximately *15,003.98* units.

2.4.3   AI in Supply Chain Optimization

AI helps optimize the supply chain using predictive analytics to forecast demand and manage inventory. By doing so, the businesses can minimize the costs while making sure that the products are available.

If $C(t)$ is the total cost of managing the inventory over time t and the inventory includes the following costs $H(Q)$, ordering costs $O(Q)$, and stockout costs $S(Q)$, where Q is the inventory quantity, the total cost is given by Eq. (2.23)

$$C(t) = H(Q) + O(Q) + S(Q) \tag{2.23}$$

Optimizing Inventory Costs:
To minimize total costs, we differentiate $C(Q)$ with respect to Q and set it to zero to find the optimal order quantity Q^*

$$\frac{dC}{dQ} = 0$$

This helps identify the inventory level that minimizes total costs.
Total Cost over Time:
To compute the total cost over a period from $t = 0$ to T, we use Eq. (2.24):

$$C_{total} = \int_0^T C(t).dt \tag{2.24}$$

Equation (2.24) gives the overall cost of maintaining inventory over time.

Example:
A retailer uses AI to optimize its inventory management. The total cost of holding and ordering inventory is modeled as $C(Q) = 200 + 100Q - 2Q^2$, where $Q = 50$ is the order quantity. Find the optimal order quantity Q^* that minimizes the total cost, and calculate the total cost savings over time.
   Step 1: Find Q^*:
   To find the optimal order quantity Q^*

$$\frac{dC(Q)}{dQ} = 0$$

Thus,

$$\frac{d(200 + 100Q - 2Q^2)}{dQ} = 100 - 4Q = 0$$

$Q^* = 25$ units

Step 2: Compute Cost Savings:

As the original order quantity was $Q = 50$, the original cost is:

$$C(Q) = 200 + 100Q - 2Q^2 = C(50) = 200 + 100.50 - 2(50)^2 = 1450$$

Step 3: Calculate the Total Cost at the Optimal Order Quantity:

Substitute $Q^* = 25$ into the cost function:

$$C(Q) = 200 + 100Q - 2Q^2 = C(25) = 200 + 100.25 - 2(25)^2 = 950$$

Thus, the total cost savings by optimizing inventory is $1450 - 950 = 500$.

2.4.4 AI in Customer Experience Personalization

AI uses machine learning algorithms to assess customer behavior and provide tailored suggestions, hence increasing customer satisfaction. Personalization algorithms use past data to strengthen marketing campaigns and forecast customer preferences.

Due to level of personalization P due to AI, customer satisfaction is denoted by $C(P)$, and can be modeled by Eq. (2.25)

$$C(P) = a + bP \tag{2.25}$$

where a is the base customer satisfaction and b is the contribution of personalization.

Thus, the rate of change in customer satisfaction can be given by Eq. (2.26)

$$\frac{dC}{dP} = b \tag{2.26}$$

Equation (2.26) indicates that as level of personalization increases, customer satisfaction improves linearly.

Total customer satisfaction over a time period from $t = 0$ to T is given by Eq. (2.27)

$$C_{total} = \int_0^T C(P(t)).dt \qquad (2.27)$$

If personalization increases over time at $P(t) = k. t$, then the total customer satisfaction becomes

$$C_{total} = \int_0^T (a + b.kt).dt = aT + \frac{bkT^2}{2}$$

Example:
A streaming service uses AI to personalize movie recommendations; customer satisfaction is mathematically modeled as $C(P) = 80 + 5P$, where P is the level of personalization, which increases at $p(t) = 0.5t$ over time. Find customer satisfaction over a 10-month period.

Step 1: Define the customer satisfaction function
Using Eq. (2.25), we get

$$C(P) = a + bP = 80 + 5P = 80 + 5(0.5)t = 80 + 2.5t$$

Step 2: Total Customer Satisfaction over 10-month period
Using Eq. (2.27)

$$C_{total} = \int_0^T C(P(t)).dt = \int_0^{10} (80 + 2.5t).dt = 925$$

Thus, the total customer satisfaction is 925 units.

2.4.5 AI in Cost Reduction Through Automation

AI reduces operational costs by automating complicated processes and optimizes resource allocation. Cost reductions from AI may be predicted and measured over time.

If C(t) be the cost of business process and it decreases exponentially over time due to AI automation, the cost reduction over time can be modeled as in Eq. (2.28):

$$C(t) = C_0 e^{-kt} \qquad (2.28)$$

where C_0 is the initial cost, and k is the rate of cost reduction.
Total cost savings over a time period from $t = 0$ to T are given by Eq. (2.29)

$$S(T) = \int_0^T C_0 e^{-kt} \, dt = \frac{C_0}{k}\left(1 - e^{-kT}\right) \tag{2.29}$$

Equation (2.29) represents the total savings as AI automates tasks over time.

Example:
A company automates its customer service operations using AI. Initially, it costs the company 500,000/– per year. The cost decreases at a rate of 10% per year after AI implementation. Calculate the total cost savings over 5 years.

Using Eq. (2.28), we get

$$C(t) = C_0 e^{-kt} = 500{,}000.e^{-0.10t}$$

To find the total cost savings over 5 years, we use Eq. (2.29)

$$S(T) = \int_0^T C_0 e^{-kt} \, dt = \int_0^5 500{,}000.e^{-0.10t} \, dt = 1{,}967{,}500/ -$$

Thus, the total cost savings over 5 years are 1,967,500/–.

2.5 Future Trends and Ethical Considerations

The fast advancement of AI enables businesses to transform their business processes. However, in addition to these advances, businesses should address ethical and regulatory challenges. While implementing AI systems, businesses should consider *AI trends, ethical issues,* and *regulatory frameworks.* By doing so, businesses will profit from AI while adhering to ethical and ethical guidelines. This section covers all the three parts in depth, with examples.

2.5.1 AI Trends

AI has swiftly altered businesses by delivering innovative methods to simplify operations, improve decision-making, enhance customer experiences, and foster development. Table 2.1 covers some of the important developments in AI for businesses, with examples.

Table 2.1 shows that AI is significantly altering the way businesses function across different sectors. Through AI-powered automation, businesses are simplifying common and repetitive processes. In predictive analytics, AI is allowing businesses to make data-driven choices by evaluating past data and anticipating future patterns, helping them comprehend customer behavior and market expectations.

Table 2.1 AI trends

AI trends	Explanation	Examples
AI-powered automation	AI-powered automation included the robotic process automation (RPA), where the repetitive and routine tasks are handled by AI	UiPath uses the RPA platform for invoice services and customer queries for companies like GE Amazon uses RPA to automate its warehouses to ensure quick delivery
AI predictive analytics	The predictive analytics uses AI to analyze the historical data and forecast trends	Netflix uses predictive analytics to recommend movies and shows based on viewing history Walmart manages its inventory to predict product demands based on the customer buying behavior Amazon uses predictive analytics as recommender systems, wherein it gives recommendations based on historical data Spotify also implements predictive analytics based on users' listening habits to create the playlist
Supply chain optimization	AI helps business to manage supply change by predicting demand. This helps business to manage inventory and rationalize logistics	DHL employs AI to manage its logistics network, forecasting delivery times and routes to ensure prompt delivery while decreasing fuel usage and transportation expenses Unilever employs AI to estimate demand for its goods, allowing it to better manage inventory and production timelines, reduce waste, and improve supply chain efficiencies
Sales and marketing	AI is being applied to boost sales and marketing by studying customer behavior, refining advertising methods, and digitizing marketing campaigns. AI in sales and marketing is referred to as predictive marketing since it predicts which customers are most inclined to purchase a product or react to a marketing message	Salesforce's Einstein AI assesses customer data and recommends the next best step for salespeople, thereby streamlining the sales process and increasing sales conversions HubSpot makes use of AI for automating marketing tasks like email advertising and social media management, reaching the appropriate consumers at the right time with tailored messaging
Financial services	AI is revolutionizing the financial services business by providing more effective fraud detection, credit rating, and automated trading. AI algorithms examine massive information to find trends, anticipate risks, and automate financial decision-making	JPMorgan employs AI for contractual analysis and fraud detection, minimizing the time required to examine documentation and identify forged transactions MasterCard uses AI to identify and avoid fraud in real time through investigating transaction data and detecting suspect patterns

(continued)

Table 2.1   (continued)

AI trends	Explanation	Examples
Healthcare	AI is transforming healthcare by assisting in diagnosis, personalizing therapies, and optimizing hospital operations. AI-powered tools examine medical data, assist doctors in making accurate choices, and offer higher quality treatments	IBM Watson examines medical records, clinical study, and patient data to help doctors in discovering and curing diseases Zebra uses AI to examine medical images data (such as X-rays) to identify diseases faster and with better accuracy
Human resources and recruitment	AI tools simplify the employment process, scan prospects according to established criteria, and even examine employee performance to predict turnover or recommend customized strategies for growth	HireVue applies AI in evaluating prospects through video interviews, studying facial movements, voice, and vocabulary selection to prioritize prospective employees Pymetrics applies AI and neuroscience-based tests to rate prospective employees' cognition and emotive attributes, aligning them to acceptable job tasks without human bias
Manufacturing and Industry 4.0	The merging of AI in manufacturing, frequently referred to as Industry 4.0, where AI and data-driven systems assist in improving output processes. AI-powered systems observe machinery, identify possible breakdowns, and optimize product quality	Siemens employs AI in its production facilities to forecast equipment maintenance requirements, avoiding downtime by resolving problems before they become significant. The technology collects sensor data from equipment and utilizes predictive analytics to warn potential complications GE employs AI in its industrial processes to maximize production schedules, eliminate waste, and ensure uniform product quality across its plants globally

Supply chain optimization is another significant area where AI is having an impact, helping businesses to forecast demand, manage inventories, and improve logistical operations. AI is also transforming sales and marketing by automating campaigns, evaluating customer needs, and improving advertising methods to reach the appropriate audience at the right time. In the financial sector, AI helps fraud detection, simplifying financial decisions and strengthening risk management. Healthcare is benefitting from AI via better diagnosis, individualized treatment plans, and streamlined hospital operations, boosting the quality of patient care. In human resources, AI is being used to simplify recruiting procedures, measure employee performance, and decrease bias in hiring. Finally, in manufacturing and Industry 4.0, AI is improving production processes, forecasting maintenance requirements, and ensuring product quality. Overall, AI is driving creativity, enhancing operational efficiency, and helping businesses to be more flexible and agile in today's environment.

2.5.2 Ethical Issues with AI

As AI continues to revolutionize the way businesses operate, it also raises certain ethical issues. The role AI takes in businesses such as automating processes, evaluating customer data, optimizing supply chains, and making decisions might also unwittingly perpetuate biasness, infringe on privacy, and cause transparency problems. Additionally, the loss of employment, uneven access to AI technology, and lack of accountability in decision-making further underline the need for ethical principles. Table 2.2 lists the ethical concerns for the benefits listed in Table 2.1, highlighting the ethical issues that accompany each advantage of AI adoption.

From Table 2.2, we recognized the ethical issues of deploying AI in many sectors (albeit the sectors examined are not comprehensive). It was discovered that the ethical issues in each sector varied greatly, necessitating specific techniques to solve these challenges successfully. The solutions presented in Table 2.2 are broad and general in nature, and it is the obligation of businesses adopting AI technology to either accept the proposed approaches or build customized methods that correspond with their unique ethical concerns. However, the answers alone may not be adequate to entirely reduce ethical issues. There is also a significant requirement for regulatory compliance, which guarantees that AI deployment follows legal frameworks and ethical norms, a subject we shall discuss in the last part of this section.

2.5.3 Regulatory Frameworks for AI Implementation

As businesses use AI technology, it is vital to ensure that these systems are being implemented correctly and in accordance with regulations. Several regulatory frameworks give norms to improve transparency, fairness, privacy, and accountability in AI systems. In this part, we will study significant regulatory frameworks and relate them to the sectors outlined in Table 2.2. Table 2.3 addresses the extant regulatory frameworks, explaining its scope, relevance to AI, and the specific sectors to which they should be applicable. Table 2.3 demonstrates how different regulations manage critical issues such as data privacy, transparency, and accountability in AI applications, ensuring businesses across diverse sectors comply with ethical and legal requirements while deploying AI technology. We need to further relate the regulatory compliances described in Table 2.3 to the particular sectors which are detailed in Table 2.4.

Table 2.2 Ethical issues of AI

AI trends	Ethical issues	Possible solution
AI-powered automation	*Job displacement:* AI automation might lead to employment loss as technology takes over conventional and repetitive jobs	Companies should invest in training and reskilling to better prepare them for tasks with greater complexity that demand human judgment and ingenuity, concentrating on human–AI cooperation rather than substitution
AI predictive analytics	*Privacy concerns:* AI typically analyzes enormous volumes of personal data to develop predictions. *Data bias and manipulation:* Personalization may lead to echo chambers because customers are only presented what matches with their previous actions, restricting exposure to innovative thoughts	For privacy concerns, businesses must secure data privacy by anonymizing personal data, gaining informed consent, and adhering to privacy legislation Regarding data bias and manipulation: To minimize over-personalization, businesses should adopt diversity algorithms that expose customers to a greater variety of products, services, and information
Supply chain optimization	*Environmental impact:* Optimizing supply chains using AI may result in increased consumption rates and resource deterioration	Ensure AI improves supply chains with an emphasis on environmentalism, leveraging data to decrease waste, minimize carbon footprints, and promote sustainable resource usage
Sales and marketing	*Manipulation and trust:* AI in marketing might sway customers into making purchase choices they wouldn't ordinarily make	Adopt ethical marketing approaches that concentrate on empowering customers with knowledge and accessibility. AI should aid customers instead of persuading them into undesired purchasing
Financial services	*Bias in decision-making:* AI algorithms applied for credit scoring or fraud detection may propagate biases, disproportionately impacting specific sections	Ensure algorithmic fairness by employing diverse training datasets and performing frequent bias checks to avoid biased results in financial services
Healthcare	*Informed consent and transparency:* Patients may not completely comprehend how AI is being employed in their healthcare choice	Healthcare companies must provide truthful communications regarding AI's involvement in diagnoses and treatment Patients should offer informed consent and have the opportunity to opting out of AI-driven healthcare
Human resources and recruitment	*Discrimination:* AI algorithms employed in recruiting might inadvertently add bias, resulting to unethical hiring practices	Use bias-mitigation approaches in AI models, such as training the system using different datasetsRegularly perform fairness validation to confirm AI is making unbiased hiring choices
Manufacturing and Industry 4.0	Job displacement and possible workplace risks owing to autonomous machines	Emphasis on human–machine collaboration, allowing employees new responsibilities in monitoring AI-powered technologies

Table 2.3 Established regulatory frameworks

Regulatory framework	Scope	Relevance to AI
General Data Protection Regulation (GDPR)	The GDPR is the most stringent data privacy standards internationally. It controls how businesses collect, handle, store, and distribute personal data, safeguarding people' privacy rights	Any AI system that handles sensitive information (e.g., customer data, user behavior) must be compliant with GDPR, notably in areas like informed consent, right to be forgotten, and data minimization
Artificial Intelligence Act	The EU's Artificial Intelligence Act is intended at regulating AI based on a risk assessment methodology. AI systems are classed into classifications such as unacceptable risk, high risk, limited risk, and minimal risk	AI applications, including those in biometric identity, critical facilities, and healthcare, are deemed high risk and have stricter restrictions
Health Insurance Portability and Accountability Act (HIPAA)	HIPAA oversees the application and dissemination of health information in the USA. It is applicable to healthcare organizations, insurance companies, and any of the AI systems that handle medical information	AI systems for healthcare (e.g., diagnostic tools, patient data management systems) must conform to HIPAA's requirements on data security, privacy, and patient rights
California Consumer Privacy Act (CCPA)	The CCPA concentrates on offering California citizens greater control over their personal data. It encompasses the right to know what information is being collected and the right to seek its erasure	Any AI system that handles data from California citizens must be compliant with CCPA, ensuring transparency, data protection, and erasure rights
Algorithmic Accountability Act	The compliance proposes to compel businesses to audit and review their AI systems for bias, fairness, and transparency. It pertains to any automated decision-making system, especially ones with considerable social or economic impact	AI systems in financial services, recruiting, and healthcare would require frequent assessments for fairness and to prevent bias
Ethical AI Guidelines	Several countries, like Australia, Canada, and Singapore, have created ethical AI frameworks that encourage responsible application of AI. The regulations promote trust, safety, transparency, and fairness	AI implementations in sectors such as retail, banking, and customer service are encouraged to comply with these ethical criteria to develop confidence and maintain accountability in AI-driven decisions

Table 2.4 Linking sectors with regulatory frameworks

Sector	Regulations	Compliance
AI-powered automation	GDPR, Ethical AI Guidelines	Automation systems that process personal data must adhere to GDPR to guarantee data security. Ethical AI principles have to be adhered to reduce job losses
AI in predictive analytics	GDPR, Algorithmic Accountability Act	Predictive analytics models that use sensitive information must comply with GDPR. The Algorithmic Accountability Act requires audits to verify that forecasts about customer behavior or market trends are accurate and equitable
Supply chain optimization	Ethical AI Guidelines, GDPR	AI models for supply chain optimization that use personal information (e.g., customer orders) must be compliant with GDPR. Ethical principles must be observed to maintain a viable supply chain
Sales and marketing	GDPR, CCPA	AI systems that examine data from customers for marketing strategies must comply with data protection rules such as GDPR and CCPA in order to secure customer information
Financial services	Algorithmic Accountability Act, Ethical AI Guidelines	According to the Algorithmic Accountability Act, financial AI systems used for credit scoring or fraud detection must be audited on a regular basis to ensure their fairness and bias
Healthcare	HIPAA, GDPR	AI systems that manage healthcare data must follow HIPAA and GDPR regulations to ensure patient data privacy and security, as well as gain explicit permission for data processing
Human resources and recruitment	Algorithmic Accountability Act, GDPR	AI-powered recruiting tools must prevent disproportionate outcomes and adhere to GDPR by handling potential employees' data transparently and safely
Manufacturing and Industry 4.0	Ethical AI Guidelines, Algorithmic Accountability Act	AI-powered manufacturing processes ought to conform to ethical standards to provide transparency, safety, and human supervision

Exercises

Exercise 1: Majid Al Futtaim's AI-Driven Transformation

1. Introduction

Majid Al Futtaim, a UAE-based conglomerate operating in retail, leisure, and real estate, has adopted AI to enhance customer experiences and improve operational efficiency.

2. Company Overview

Majid Al Futtaim formed in 1992 and now works in 16 countries spanning the Middle East, Africa, and Asia. The company's operations comprise shopping malls, retail, hotels, leisure, and entertainment. To remain competitive in a fast-changing industry, Majid Al Futtaim used AI solutions across all business sectors to boost operational efficiency and customer engagement.

3. How Majid Al Futtaim Uses AI

3.1 AI for Retail (Carrefour)

- Majid Al Futtaim's Carrefour retail stores in the UAE use AI for a number of purposes, including tailored marketing, inventory management, and customer service. Some important areas where AI is used include:
  Tailored shopping experience: AI-powered algorithms evaluate the customer shopping behavior and deliver tailored suggestions and deals, hence increasing customer engagement.
- Automated inventory management: AI forecasts customer demand using past data, market trends, and sales patterns. This guarantees that Carrefour stores possess the correct items, eliminating waste and stockouts.

3.2 Artificial Intelligence in Shopping Malls (Mall of the Emirates)

AI is being used at Majid Al Futtaim's shopping Malls to improve the tourist experience. For example:

- Smart parking systems: AI-powered parking systems point customers toward available parking spaces, decreasing time wasted searching for parking
- Customer journey analytics: AI watches visitors and customer behavior across the mall, allowing businesses to optimize store layouts and enhance overall customer experience.

3.3 AI in Cinema and Leisure (VOX Cinemas)

Majid Al Futtaim's VOX Cinemas use AI to improve the movie-going experience by:

- Predictive analytics for movie preferences: AI algorithms use customer information for suggesting movies based on their own preferences.
- AI-powered chatbots: AI-powered chatbots help customers with queries, reservations, and service requests, delivering 24-h customer care.

  Task: Analyze how AI has improved Majid Al Futtaim's processes and outcomes.

Exercise 2:

Tata Steel, one of India's leading steel producers, has been at the forefront of using AI to automate operations and save operating costs. Faced with growing raw material prices and a highly aggressive global market, Tata Steel adopted AI across its operations to increase productivity, improve resource use, and save costs.

Overview of AI Implementation

Tata Steel used AI to automate and improve different operations across its production facilities.

Key areas where AI was used include:

1. AI systems monitor equipment health, forecast faults, and plan maintenance in advance, decreasing unexpected downtime and repair costs
2. AI improves the manufacturing process by modifying settings in real time to guarantee that resources like energy and raw materials are used efficiently
3. AI automates supply chain activities such as procurement, inventory management, and shipping, reducing inefficiencies and lowering storage costs

These AI-driven automation initiatives dramatically lowered Tata Steel's operating expenses.

Initial Costs and Cost Reduction Rate:

- Suppose the initial cost of operations before AI automation at Tata Steel is $C_0 = ₹10,000,000$ annually.
- The rate of cost reduction due to AI automation is estimated to be $k = 0.08$ per year.

Time Period:

- Tata Steel wishes to calculate its total cost savings over a period of 6 years (T=6).

Find the total cost savings over 6 years
Hint: Using Eq. (2.29)

$$S(6) = \frac{10,000,000}{0.08} \left(1 - e^{-0.08 X 6}\right) = 47,650,000$$

Thus, after 6 years, Tata Steel would have saved approximately ₹47.65 million due to AI-driven automation.

Exercise 3: AI-Driven Revenue Growth and Market Saturation in E-Commerce

QuickShop, an e-commerce startup, has incorporated AI technologies to boost revenue growth by offering personalized product recommendations and dynamic pricing strategies. These AI systems evaluate customer data in real time to provide tailored product suggestions, boost sales conversions, and automatically modify pricing depending on demand, competition, and customer profiles.

QuickShop's revenue is initially minuscule, but its business works in a big prospective market with potential for tremendous expansion. However, like with every market, its expansion is limited by market saturation and competition. QuickShop seeks to use AI to model and anticipate revenue growth over time, taking into consideration both initial quick development and subsequent market saturation.

To illustrate how AI influences QuickShop's revenue growth, consider the following parameters:

- Initial revenue, $R_0 = 10,000$
- Market limit, $K = 100,000$
- Growth rate constant, $\alpha = 0.01$ *per year*
- Time period, $t = 5$ *years*

Find how much revenue is projected to grow after 5 years for QuickShop with the implementation of AI.

Hint: Using Eq. (2.3), we get

$$R(5) = \frac{100,000}{1 + \left(\frac{100,000 - 10,000}{10,000}\right)e^{-0.1*5}} = 15,480.94$$

Thus, after 5 years, the revenue of the company will be 15,480.94, and will continue till the limiting factor, $K = 100,000$.

References

Al-Hashimi, H. M. (2023). Turing, von Neumann, and the computational architecture of biological machines. *Proceedings of the National Academy of Sciences of the United States of America, 120*(25), e2220022120. https://doi.org/10.1073/pnas.2220022120

Borowiec, S. (2016). Google's AI machine v world champion of "Go": Everything you need to know. *The Guardian.* https://www.theguardian.com/technology/2016/mar/09/googles-ai-machine-v-world-champion-of-go-everything-you-need-to-know

Dick, S. (2019). Artificial intelligence. *Harvard Data Science Review, 1*(1). https://doi.org/10.1162/99608f92.92fe150c

Emmert-Streib, F., Yang, Z., Feng, H., Tripathi, S., & Dehmer, M. (2020). An introductory review of deep learning for prediction models with big data. *Frontiers in Artificial Intelligence, 3*, 4. https://doi.org/10.3389/frai.2020.00004

Garikapati, D., & Shetiya, S. S. (2024). Autonomous vehicles: Evolution of artificial intelligence and the current industry landscape. *Big Data and Cognitive Computing, 8*(4), Article 4. https://doi.org/10.3390/bdcc8040042

Gatera, A. (2024). Role of artificial intelligence in revenue management and pricing strategies in hotels. *Journal of Modern Hospitality, 3*, 14–25. https://doi.org/10.47941/jmh.1957

Gugerty, L. (2006). Newell and Simon's logic theorist: Historical background and impact on cognitive modeling. *Proceedings of the Human Factors and Ergonomics Society Annual Meeting, 50*, 880–884. https://doi.org/10.1177/154193120605000904

Haleem, A., Javaid, M., Qadri, M. A., Singh, R. P., & Suman, R. (2022). Artificial intelligence (AI) applications for marketing: A literature-based study. *International Journal of Intelligent Networks, 3*, 119–132. https://doi.org/10.1016/j.ijin.2022.08.005

Islam, J., Vasant, P., Negash, B., Laruccia, M., Myint, M., & Watada, J. (2020). A holistic review on artificial intelligence techniques for well placement optimization problem. *Advances in Engineering Software, 141*, 102767. https://doi.org/10.1016/j.advengsoft.2019.102767

Jiang, Y., Li, X., Luo, H., Yin, S., & Kaynak, O. (2022). Quo vadis artificial intelligence? *Discover Artificial Intelligence, 2*(1), 4. https://doi.org/10.1007/s44163-022-00022-8

Medium. (2023, October 7). How Netflix uses AI to personalize content recommendations and improve digital.... *Medium*. https://medium.com/@shizk/case-study-how-netflix-uses-ai-to-personalize-content-recommendations-and-improve-digital-b253d08352fd

Parsons, L. (2020, October 26). Ethical concerns mount as AI takes bigger decision-making role. *Harvard Gazette*. https://news.harvard.edu/gazette/story/2020/10/ethical-concerns-mount-as-ai-takes-bigger-decision-making-role/

Rafiq, F. (2023, June 29). The emergence of virtual assistants and voice recognition technology. *Women in Technology*. https://medium.com/womenintechnology/the-emergence-of-virtual-assistants-and-voice-recognition-technology-eb94140cd310

Toews, R. (2019). To understand the future of AI, study its past. *Forbes*. https://www.forbes.com/sites/robtoews/2019/11/17/to-understand-the-future-of-ai-study-its-past/

Toosi, A., Bottino, A., Saboury, B., & Rahmim, A. (2021). A brief history of AI: How to prevent another winter (a critical review). *PET Clinics, 16*. https://doi.org/10.1016/j.cpet.2021.07.001

Turing, A. M. (1950). Computing machinery and intelligence. *Mind, 59*, 433–460. https://doi.org/10.1093/mind/LIX.236.433

Vadlamani, S. K., Xiao, T. P., & Yablonovitch, E. (2020). Physics successfully implements Lagrange multiplier optimization. *Proceedings of the National Academy of Sciences of the United States of America, 117*(43), 26639–26650. https://doi.org/10.1073/pnas.2015192117

Werbos, P. (1988). *Backpropagation: Past and future* (*I*, Vol. 1, pp. 343–353). https://doi.org/10.1109/ICNN.1988.23866

Yoon, V. Y., & Adya, M. (2003). *Expert systems construction* (pp. 291–300). https://doi.org/10.1016/B0-12-227240-4/00068-X

Chapter 3
Exploring Blockchain Technology

Abstract This chapter explores the revolutionary potential of blockchain technology, following its development from the early days of Bitcoin to its present use in a multitude of sectors. The chapter examines the fundamental elements of blockchain, including nodes, chains, and blocks, and provides mathematical models that describe broadcasting and transaction validation in decentralized networks. The chapter also looks at how blockchain can affect the economy, emphasizing how it could reduce costs, increase revenue, and manage risks. The chapter also addresses ethical issues including data privacy, legal compliance, and the environmental effects of blockchain's consensus processes, as well as future trends like blockchain interoperability, AI integration, and sustainability.

Keywords Blockchain technology · Distributed ledger · Smart contracts · Economic impact · Interoperability · AI integration · Risk management · Sustainability · Decentralization

3.1 Introduction

Blockchain has evolved as a disruptive technology and revolutionized the way data and transactions are stored and authenticated. This chapter explains the nuances of blockchain technology for businesses. The chapter is divided into five sections, wherein Sect. 3.2 gives the history of blockchain and outlines its evolution through four distinct phases. Section 3.3 describes fundamental components of blockchain, including blocks, chains, and nodes, and offers a mathematical explanation of how transaction and data are stored and validated in the blockchain. Section 3.4 gives the economic advantages of blockchain with reference to costs, risks, and revenue. The section also uses several examples to explain the economic implications of blockchain. The final section, Sect. 3.5, explores the future trends and regulatory requirements of implementing blockchain for businesses.

3.2   History and Evolution of Blockchain Technology

Blockchain technology, introduced with Bitcoin in 2008, has subsequently matured into a breakthrough technology with applicability across different sectors. Its *decentralized, transparent, immutable,* and *secure* structure has made it a transformational technology. The section explores the history and growth of blockchain technology, from its creation to present.

Initial Development: 2008–2010
Blockchain's journey started in 2008 with the creation of Bitcoin by the fictitious character Satoshi Nakamoto, who released the whitepaper "*Bitcoin: A Peer-to-Peer Electronic Cash System*" (Nakamoto, 2008) describing a decentralized digital currency that operates without intermediaries such as banks. The underlying technology of Bitcoin was blockchain, a distributed ledger which stores transactions in a transparent and tamper-proof manner. Key properties of blockchain includes decentralization (with no central authority controlling the network), transparency (enabling all participants to see transaction history), and immutability (ensuring that once a transaction has been recorded, it cannot be edited or deleted). In January 2009, Nakamoto mined the first Bitcoin block, known as the Genesis Block, indicating the start of blockchain technology (Ducrée, 2022). The first block reward of 50 BTC per block pushed miners to participate in the decentralized system.

Blockchain 1.0
Blockchain technology was associated with Bitcoin and other cryptocurrencies throughout the Blockchain 1.0 period (2010–2014), primarily serving as the foundation for digital currencies. As Bitcoin gained popularity, a number of other cryptocurrencies, or "altcoins," surfaced. These included Litecoin (2011), which sought to provide faster transactions, Ripple (2012), which was intended to facilitate immediate cross-border payments, and Peercoin (2013), which introduced a hybrid consensus mechanism combining Proof-of-Stake and Proof-of-Work. Although Bitcoin demonstrated the promise of blockchain technology, its weaknesses were made clear, especially with regard to scalability (Herrera-Joancomartí & Pérez-Solà, 2016); its network could only process around seven transactions per second (TPS) (Kwaasteniet, 2019), which meant that it was not appropriate for high-volume transaction systems. Additionally, during this phase, blockchain's uses were primarily constrained to peer-to-peer financial transactions, exposing its constraining functionality (Duan et al., 2023).

Blockchain 2.0
Blockchain 2.0 began in 2015 with the creation of Ethereum, which extended blockchain beyond cryptocurrency, and introduced smart contracts and decentralized applications (dApps) (Vujičić et al., 2018). Ethereum, which was first introduced by Vitalik Buterin, enables developers to design self-executing

contracts, in which the conditions of the agreement are encoded into the code, so enabling trustless transactions (called smart contracts) (Sklaroff, 2017). A Turing-complete language allowed for the development of a wide range of dApps and automated smart contracts that did away with the need for intermediaries. The projects like CryptoKitties in 2017 demonstrated how digital assets could be handled on the blockchain, and platforms like MakerDAO and Uniswap, which decentralized financial operations, led to development of Decentralized Finance (DeFi). However, Blockchain 2.0 was hampered by issues like scalability [as Ethereum can only execute 15–20 transactions per second (TPS)] and energy consumption (both Bitcoin and Ethereum use a Proof-of-Work consensus mechanism, which uses a lot of energy) (Alzoubi & Mishra, 2023).

Blockchain 3.0

The Blockchain 3.0 (2018–present) has seen a steady development in blockchain technology, overcoming the constraint of scalability (Jasim & Hadi, 2023). Innovations such as Proof-of-Stake (PoS) are being implemented to address scalability difficulties; Ethereum moved from Proof-of-Work to energy-efficient consensus method with Ethereum 2.0 (Brittany, 2022). Furthermore, by processing transactions off-chain, Layer 2 solutions like Plasma and Lightning Network improve scalability, and sharding divides the network into smaller portions to enable parallel transaction processing. During this phase, apart from finance, blockchain is now being used in supply chain management (e.g., Walmart and IBM use it to track products and guarantee food safety); healthcare (e.g., MedRec provides secure storage and access to medical records); government (e.g., Estonia uses blockchain to verify digital identities securely); financial services (e.g., JPMorgan streamlines transactions); and central banks [e.g., Central Bank Digital Currencies (CBDCs)]. With this progression, blockchain's potential has also extended.

Blockchain 4.0

Blockchain 4.0 has an array of applications that will likely influence how technology evolves in the future. There are blockchains that work independently, interoperability between blockchain is now becoming important; and initiatives like Polkadot and Cosmos are striving to enable smooth communication and data transfer across various blockchains. Hybrid blockchains are also becoming prevalent which combines the security and control of private blockchains with the transparency of public blockchains. Also, Decentralized Autonomous Organizations (DAOs) are upending conventional company structures by using smart contracts to redefine corporate governance. Furthermore, the blend of blockchain and AI is poised to transform the development of secure and efficient decentralized AI networks. Collectively, these developments demonstrate the disruptive potential of blockchain technology across different sectors, offering greater interoperability, security, and new organizational structures.

3.3   Blockchain Technology and Distributed Ledger Systems

Blockchain technology and distributed ledger systems are the latest tools that have revolutionized the way the business data get stored and disseminated. Blockchain actually serves as a digital ledger that is accessed and verified by multiple computers, providing a secure and transparent method to record data. The important characteristic of blockchain technology is that once data gets recorded in the block, it cannot be modified or altered, thereby guaranteeing the authenticity and veracity of the data. The section provides a step-by-step explanation of how blockchain works.

There are five steps to explain the detailed working of blockchain:

Step 1: Transaction Initiation
The user of blockchain is called *Node*. A transaction is initiated by user (we call *Node A*). This transaction can be either transfer of value (cryptocurrency) or data (can be smart contract). This can be shown by Eq. (3.1)

$$[Node\ A] \rightarrow [Transaction\ Data] \tag{3.1}$$

If *Node A* wants to transfer x value, then $f(x)$ is the transaction fee, which is calculated as percentage of x.

Thus, if fees are 1% then $f(x) = 1\ \%\ of\ x = 0.01.\ x$

If T represents the amount that needs to be transferred after deducting the transaction fee, then

$$T = x - f(x) \tag{3.2}$$

where T is thus the final transaction cost.

Thus, if *Node A* wants to transfer $x = 100$ units

$$\therefore f(x) = 1\%of\ x = 0.01\ X\ 100 = 1 \text{ unit of transaction fee}$$

$$T = 100 - 1 = 99 \text{ units}$$

Thus, 99 units to be transferred to recipient from sender, *Node A*.

Step 2: Transaction Broadcast to Network
The transaction is then broadcasted to all the nodes in the blockchain network as mentioned by Eq. (3.3)

$$[Transaction\ Data] \rightarrow [Network\ Nodes] \tag{3.3}$$

So, if there are N nodes in the network, then the transaction T (*from step* 1) is broadcasted to all N nodes. This is called as *total broadcasting effort*. The transaction *T* resides in mempool of each node in the network. This can be mathematically stated by Eq. (3.4)

$$Broadcast(T) = T \; X \; N \tag{3.4}$$

If $N = 1000$ nodes

$$Broadcast(T) = 99 \; X \; 1000 = 99{,}000.$$

Thus, 99,000 units of effort (or process) are needed throughout the network for the transaction to be broadcasted to all 1000 nodes. This demonstrates how broadcasting a single transaction may result in enormous processing effort, particularly as blockchain networks multiply in size. In order to avoid processing effort, some blockchain networks employ optimizations like sharding or Layer 2 solutions (e.g., Lightning Network) to lower the overall broadcasting efforts and make the network more scalable.

For our discussion, we will assume that we require 99,000 units of processing to broadcast the transaction.

Step 3: Transaction Broadcast to Network
In step 3, after the transaction has been broadcasted to the network, there are nodes in the network that validate the transactions. These nodes are called *Miners*. The validation ensures that the transaction is legitimate and, thus, can be added to the blockchain.

$$[Mempool] \rightarrow [Transaction \; T] \rightarrow [Validation \; process]$$

If the balance of *Node A* is B_a and the transaction amount is T_a(excluding the transaction fees), then miner nodes perform the validation process. The validation is approved as mentioned by Eq. (3.5)

$$B_a > T_a \tag{3.5}$$

Example: If $B_a = 150$ and $T_a = 99$, then $150 \geq 99$, the transaction can proceed, otherwise not.

Furthermore, the digital signature of the transaction is verified to ensure that the transaction is initiated by legitimate node.

To verify the digital signature, we need to understand the complete process for Node A

$$Transaction \; Data = T$$

Transaction *T* is passed through hash function to generate hash value *H(T)*. Hash function is the fixed size representation of transaction T and is unique fingerprint of the transaction and is represented by Eq. (3.6)

$$H(T) = hash\ (T) \tag{3.6}$$

$$[Transaction\ Data\ T] \rightarrow [Hash\ function\ h(T)] \rightarrow [hash\ value\ H(T)]$$

Then, $H(T)$ is signed by the private key of *Node A*, and a digital signature $\sigma(T)$ is generated, mentioned in Eq. (3.7).

$$\sigma(T) = Encrypt(H(T), SK_a) \tag{3.7}$$

where SK_a is private key of *Node A*.

This can be represented as

$$[Hash\ Value\ H(T)] \rightarrow [Private\ Key, SK_a] \rightarrow [Digital\ Signature, \sigma(T)]$$

This digital signature $\sigma(T)$ is attached to the transaction data T and broadcast to the network as given in Eq. (3.8)

$$[Transaction\ Data\ (T)] + [Digital\ Signature, \sigma(T)] \tag{3.8}$$

To decrypt the nodes in the blockchain network, we use the public key of *Node A*, PK_a to decrypt the digital signature $\sigma(T)$, as given by Eq. (3.9)

$$H(T') = Decrypt(\sigma(T), PK_a) \tag{3.9}$$

After decrypting the digital signature, the nodes get the hash value T. If $H(T') = H(T)$, digital signature is verified and transaction is authentic and can be added to the blockchain. The authentication is shown in Eq. (3.10)

$$Validate\ \sigma(T) = \begin{cases} 1, if\ H(T') = H(T) \\ 0, if\ H(T') \neq H(T) \end{cases} \tag{3.10}$$

This process ensures that the transaction is secure, authentic, and legitimate.

Step 4: Transaction Grouping into block

In step 4, once all the transactions are validated by the miner node, the aim is to group all these transactions into a block. This block will be eventually added to the blockchain once it is verified by consensus mechanism.

Consensus mechanism requires miners to use Proof-of-Work (*PoW*). *PoW* requires miners to solve cryptographic puzzle and find a special number, called nonce. The hash of nonce when combined with all the transactions $(T_1, T_2, \ldots . T_n)$ and the hash of the previous block (H_{prev}) should be less than target difficulty level D.

Mathematically, it can be denoted by Eq. (3.11)

$$H(Block\ Header) = \{H_{prev}\|T_1\|T_2\|\ldots\ldots\ldots\|T_n\|timestamp\|N\} \qquad (3.11)$$

The process repeats till one of the miner node satisfies the condition $H(Block\ Header) < D$.

The blockchain sets the target difficulty level D using the following steps:

1) Expected time for last difficulty period:
   So, the expected time for 2016 blocks is 10 min.
   Thus, $T_{expected} = 2016\ X\ 10 = 20,160$ min
2) Actual time taken for the last difficulty period T_{actual} to mine 2016 blocks.
3) Calculate the adjustment factor, $A = \frac{T_{actual}}{T_{expected}}$
4) Adjust the difficulty, $D_{new} = D_{current}\ X\ A$
5) Limits of adjustment:
   To prevent extreme change, the bitcoin caps the adjustment factor to be within four times (up or down) the previous difficulty. Thus, the range of adjustment factor A is $0.25 \leq A \leq 4$.

Once, the miner satisfies the condition $H(Block\ Header) < D$, the creation of block (with all the transactions) can be expressed as given by Eq. (3.12)

$$B = \sum_{i=1}^{n} T_i \qquad (3.12)$$

Thus, blockchain C is updated by appending new block B

$$C = C + B$$

So, if N is the number of nodes in the blockchain, the distributed ledger is

$$l = C\ X\ N$$

where C is the updated blockchain and ensures consistency.

Also, once the block is added to the network, the first miner node who adds block to blockchain gets rewarded for its efforts in validating and adding a new block to the blockchain.

The reward includes block reward and transaction fees from all the transactions included in the block.

Mathematical representation of miner reward is shown in Eq. (3.13)

$$T_R = R + F \qquad (3.13)$$

where R is the block reward and F is the sum of each transaction fee, $f(T_i)$,
$F = \sum_{i=1}^{n} f(T_i)$

Thus, Eq. (3.13) can be rewritten as in Eq. (3.14)

$$T_R = R + \sum_{i=1}^{n} f(T_i) \qquad (3.14)$$

Step 5: Confirmation and Finality
The finality of a transaction refers to the probability that the transaction cannot be reversed, and the probability that the block cannot be altered as more blocks are added to the network.

If the attacker wants to reverse the transaction, they need to re-mine the block containing the transaction.

The probability that the attacker successfully re-mines the block$=p$.
The probability that honest node mines the block is $q = 1 - p$.

Thus, for n blocks,

The probability that the attacker successfully re-mines all the n blocks is p^n.
The probability that attacker fails to re-mine all n blocks is $1 - p^n$.

We assume that both attacker and honest miner have equal hash power, which means that there is 50% chance $\cong \frac{1}{2}$.
Probability of re-mining n blocks

$$p^n = \left(\frac{1}{2}\right) X \left(\frac{1}{2}\right) X \dots \dots \dots X \left(\frac{1}{2}\right) (n \ times)$$

$$p^n = \left(\frac{1}{2}\right)^n = \frac{1}{2^n}$$

Thus, the probability that transaction remains confirmed and is given by Eq. (3.15)

$$P(n) = 1 - p^n = 1 - \frac{1}{2^n} \qquad (3.15)$$

Example:
Thus, the probability of a transaction remaining confirmed after $n = 6 \ blocks$

$$P(6) = 1 - \frac{1}{2^6} = 0.984375$$

So, after six blocks, there is 98.43% chance that the transaction is irreversible.

3.4   Economic Impact of Blockchain

Blockchain technology has transformed how businesses interact with customers and to handle transactions. As blockchain deals with two important elements of business—customers and transactions, it is critical to determine the economic viability of deploying blockchain technology. The three economic criteria are considered are *cost reduction*, *revenue management*, and *risk assessment*, which demonstrates that blockchain not only simplifies business processes but also reduces the cost and risk.

3.4.1   Cost Reduction

Blockchain significantly reduces business expenditures like *transaction*, *operational*, and *compliance* costs.

a)   *Transaction costs*

Blockchain processes transaction continuously, and the transaction costs also include the marginal cost per transactions $MC(t)$. By using blockchain for transactions, $MC(t)$ decreases over time and can be given by Eq. (3.16)

$$MC(t) = MC_0.e^{-at} \tag{3.16}$$

In Eq. (3.16), MC_0 is the initial marginal costs at $t = 0$, and α is the rate at which the marginal cost decreases.

Thus, the total transaction cost for $[0, T]$ is given by Eq. (3.17)

$$TC = \int_0^T MC(t).r.dt \tag{3.17}$$

where $r.\ dt$ is the rate of transactions per unit time. The overall transaction cost thus becomes $TC[T] = \int_0^T MC_0.e^{-at}.r.dt$. Solving, we get, as shown by Eq. (3.18)

$$TC[T] = \frac{MC_0 X\ r}{\alpha}\left(1 - e^{-aT}\right) \tag{3.18}$$

b)   *Operational costs*

Blockchain automates the repetitive processes, which helps to minimize the operational costs. This can be modeled by Eq. (3.19) as

$$OC(t) = C_0.e^{-\lambda t} \tag{3.19}$$

where C_0 is the initial operational cost at $t = 0$, and λ is the rate at which the operational cost decreases.

The overall operational cost for $[0, T]$ is thus shown by Eq. (3.20)

$$OC[T] = \int_0^T C_0.e^{-\lambda t} dt = \frac{C_0}{\lambda}\left(1 - e^{-\lambda T}\right) \tag{3.20}$$

c) *Compliance costs*

Blockchain lowers compliance costs by giving real-time, immutable records, reducing the need for expensive audits and regulatory reporting. If

- C_0: Initial compliance cost.
- r: Reduction in percentage in compliance costs due to blockchain.
- $S(t)$: Compliance cost savings at time t.
- $\Delta C(t)$: Compliance cost at time t after accounting for the reduction.

There is a reduction in compliance cost $C(t)$ over time, with the reduction in % in compliance costs being r, which can be modeled as:

$$C(t) = C_0 \times (1 - r \cdot t/T) \tag{3.21}$$

The compliance cost savings at any time t can be expressed as the difference between the initial compliance costs and the compliance costs at time t, as shown by Eq. (3.22)

$$S(t) = C_0 - C(t) = C_0 \times (r \cdot t/T) \tag{3.22}$$

The total compliance cost savings for $[0, T]$ are given by Eq. (3.23)

$$\text{Total Compliance Cost Savings} = \int_0^T S(t)dt = \int_0^T C_0 \times (r \cdot t/T)dt \tag{3.23}$$

The total compliance cost savings over time due to blockchain implementation can be expressed by Eq. (3.24) as:

$$\text{Total Compliance Cost Savings } \Delta C(t) = \frac{C_0.r.T}{2} \tag{3.24}$$

Example:
   If the current compliance costs $C_0 = 120,000$, reduction percentage $r = 0.3$ (30%), and time period $T = 5$.
   Substituting these values into Eq. (3.24), we get

$$\Delta C(t) = \frac{120,000 \ X0.3 \ X \ 5}{2} = 90,000$$

Thus, the total compliance cost savings over 5 years would be *90,000 units*.

3.4.2 *Revenue Enhancement*

Blockchain opens new opportunities for businesses to generate revenue through new business models or expanding market access.

a) *New revenue streams*
   Tokenization and micropayments are two new business models enabled by blockchain technology generating additional sources of revenue for businesses. The future value of revenue streams can be analyzed using net present worth (NPV), as shown in Eq. (3.25).

$$NPV = \sum_{i=1}^{n} \frac{R_t}{(1+r)^t} - I \qquad (3.25)$$

where R_t is revenue generated in year t, r is discount rate, I is initial investment, and n are the number of years.
   Example:
   Suppose a company generates 50,000/– annually in new revenue from tokenization for 5 years, with an initial blockchain investment of 100,000/– and a discount rate of 5%. Find the future value of revenue for the business after 5 years.
   Then the future value of revenue is

$$NPV = \frac{50,000}{(1+0.05)^1} + \frac{50,000}{(1+0.05)^2} + \frac{50,000}{(1+0.05)^3} + \frac{50,000}{(1+0.05)^4} + \frac{50,000}{(1+0.05)^5}$$
$$- 100,000 = 116,473.83$$

This shows that the value of future revenue streams, discounted at 5% and less the initial investment, produces a net present value of 116,473.83/–, indicating a positive return on the blockchain investment.

b) *Increased market access*

Blockchain technology allows safe cross-border transactions, removing intermediaries, and establishing decentralized platforms for direct peer-to-peer transactions. These benefits improve market access, enabling businesses to expand into new markets.

If

- M_0 = Initial market size without blockchain,
- G = Growth rate in market size due to blockchain-driven access to new markets,
- C_b = Cost reduction percentage due to blockchain, which allows for increased cross-border transactions,
- t = Number of years,
- $V_b(t)$ = Volume of transactions or market size at time t with blockchain.

Thus, we can model the market size at time t due to blockchain adoption as shown by Eq. (3.26)

$$V_b(t) = M_0 \cdot e^{G.t} \cdot (1 - C_b) \tag{3.26}$$

In the formula, $e^{G.\ t}$ represents the exponential growth in market size over time due to globalization facilitated by blockchain, and $(1 - C_b)$ is the cost reduction factor so that more transactions to be served at lower costs.

Example:

Consider a company operates in a domestic market with an initial market size of M_0=1,000,000 transactions. The company starts using blockchain technology, which allows it to expand into international markets with the growth rate of 10%. The cost reduction due to blockchain is 20%. Find the market size after 5 years.

The market size at year 5 using Eq. (3.26) will be:

$$V_b(5) = 1,000,000 \cdot e^{0.10.5} \cdot (1 - 0.20) = 1,318,980 \text{ transactions}$$

Thus, after 5 years, the company's market size has grown to approximately 1,318,980 units, which represents a 31.9% increase in market access over the original market size.

3.4.3 Risk Management

Blockchain technology manages risks by improving security, decreasing fraud, and increasing transaction transparency. This culminates in cost savings and decreases different types of risks, including fraud and counterparty risks.

a) *Fraud reduction*

The immutability and decentralized nature of blockchains helps reduce fraud because they stop tampering with records. The Expected Value (EV) of fraud reduction can be given by Eq. (3.27):

$$EV_{fraud\ savings} = P_{fraud} \times L_{fraud} - P_{blockchain} \times L_{blockchain} \tag{3.27}$$

where

- P_{fraud} = Probability of fraud occurrence before blockchain implementation.
- L_{fraud} = Expected loss due to fraud (in monetary terms).
- $P_{blockchain}$ = Probability of fraud occurrence after blockchain implementation.
- $L_{blockchain}$ = Expected loss due to fraud after blockchain (which is typically lower than L_{fraud}.

EV represents the amount a company can save by reducing fraud through blockchain implementation. The reduction in the probability of fraud and the reduction in fraud-related losses both contribute to the total savings.

Example:

A business suffers from an estimated fraud loss of 200,000/– annually before adopting blockchain. The probability of fraud occurring is estimated to be 20%. After blockchain is implemented, the probability of fraud is reduced to 5%, and the expected loss from fraud (if it occurs) is reduced to 50,000/–. Find expected value of fraud savings.

Applying Eq. (3.27)

- $P\_fraud = 20\%$
- $L\_fraud = 100,000/-$
- $P\_blockchain = 5\%$
- $L\_blockchain = 50,000/-$

$$EV_{fraud\ savings} = 20\% \times 100,000 - 5\% \times 50,000 = 37,500/-$$

Thus, the company can expect to save 37,500/– annually by implementing blockchain to reduce fraud.

b) *Counterparty Risk Management*

Counterparty risk means the chance that the other party could default on its commitments. Blockchain lowers counterparty risk by guaranteeing reliability and transparency through decentralized, immutable records and smart contracts. These contracts autonomously implement the terms of deals without any requirement for intermediaries.

Counterparty risk mitigation can be expressed using risk-adjusted rate of return (*RAROR*) as mentioned in Eq. (3.28)

$$RAROR = \frac{R_b - R_f}{P_{default} \times L_{default} - P_{blockchain} \times L_{blockchain}} \tag{3.28}$$

where

- R_b = The increase in revenue or savings generated by implementing blockchain to reduce counterparty risk.
- R_f = The rate of return from a theoretically risk-free investment (such as government bonds).
- P_{fraud} = Probability of fraud occurrence before blockchain implementation.
- L_{fraud} = Expected loss due to fraud (in monetary terms).
- $P_{blockchain}$ = Probability of fraud occurrence after blockchain implementation.
- $L_{blockchain}$ = Expected loss due to fraud after blockchain (which is typically lower than L_{fraud}.

A higher *RAROR* implies that the investment is generating a high return for the risk concerned, whereas a lower *RAROR* would suggest that the return is lower than risk-free investments (such as government bonds).

Example:

X Pvt. Ltd deals in cross-border trade and financial agreements with foreign sellers and buyers. These types of transactions often involve long payment phases and the possibility of failure of obligations by the partners. In the past, the company has been experiencing counterparty risk in the case of default; they suffer losses due to delayed payments. To minimize counterparty risk, X Pvt. Ltd plans to adopt blockchain technology to automate and secure their commercial deals using smart contracts. This ensures that responsibilities are immediately followed and transactions are checked transparently, thus lowering the likelihood of counterparty failure. X Pvt. Ltd wants to measure the risk-adjusted return on risk (*RAROR*) after adopting blockchain to lower counterparty risk. They will compare the profits from blockchain adoption with their risk-free investment choices, such as Indian government shares or other safe investments.

- *Return from blockchain implementation*: Blockchain increases cash flow via faster payments, decreases the frequency of disputes, and cuts operational expenses owing to automation. The projected return from these benefits is calculated at ₹50,00,000 per year.
- *Risk-free rate (R_f)*: The risk-free rate in the Indian context depends on the rate of return on Government of India 10-year bonds, which is roughly 6.5% every year.
- *Probability of default before blockchain*: Before deploying blockchain, the business encountered defaults in 10% of instances

$$P_{default} = 0.10$$

- *Expected loss from default (before blockchain)*: X Pvt. Ltd. anticipates an average loss of ₹1,00,00,000 from each default in the traditional approach.
- *Probability of default after blockchain*: Following blockchain adoption, the default probability reduces to 1% because of automated smart contracts and verified transactions

$$P_{blockchain} = 0.01$$

Expected loss from default (after blockchain): Because of faster and automatic settlements, the projected loss from default lowers to ₹20,00,000.

To calculate the *RAROR*

$$R_b = ₹50,00,000$$

$$R_f = 6.5\% * ₹50,00,000 = ₹3,25,000$$

Counterparty risk before blockchain:

$$P_{default} \times L_{default} = 0.10 \times ₹1,00,00,000 = ₹10,00,000$$

Counterparty risk after blockchain:

$$P_{blockchain} \times L_{blockchain} = 0.01 \times ₹20,00,000 = ₹20,000$$

$$RAROR = \frac{50,00,000 - 3,25,000}{10,00,000 - 20,000} \approx 4.77$$

The RAROR of 4.77 suggests that for every unit of risk decreased by blockchain deployment, the business produces 4.77 times the return comparing to the risk-free investment in Indian government bonds.

3.5 Future Trends

As blockchain technology advances, there are various emerging trends and ethical implications that businesses must recognize. These developments are significant for businesses looking to effectively exploit blockchain while simultaneously resolving regulatory concerns. The three future trends in blockchain for business are sustainability, interoperability, and AI integration.

a) *Sustainability*

As blockchain evolves, the business is trying to make it sustainable by employing consensus mechanisms that require less energy, like Proof-of-Stake (*PoS*) and delegated Proof-of-Stake (*DPoS*).

Proof-of-Stake (PoS)

To demonstrate how *PoS* is sustainable, we may compare it to Proof-of-Work (*PoW*) by including the energy consumed over time.

Energy Consumption in Proof-of-Work (*PoW*)

For *PoW*, the energy consumed is equal to the processing power $P_{PoW}(t)$ and the time t spent mining blocks. The overall energy consumption E_{PoW} over the time period T is given by Eq. (3.29)

$$E_{PoW} = \int_0^T P_{PoW}(t)dt \tag{3.29}$$

In Eq. (3.29) $P_{PoW}(t)$ is the energy consumed by the miners at time t and depends on the number of miners and the difficulty level of cryptographic puzzle, and T is the total time for mining.

As difficulty of mining increases, $P_{PoW}(t)$ also increases over time.

Energy Consumption in Proof-of-Stake (PoS)

In *PoS*, validators are selected based on their position in the network, and energy usage is substantially reduced. The energy utilized by *PoS* is depending on the number of validators (N_v) and the energy necessary to validate transactions (P_{PoS}). The total energy consumption (E_{PoS}) over time T is expressed by Eq. (3.30):

$$E_{PoS} = \int_0^T N_v \, X \, P_{PoS}.dt \tag{3.30}$$

Since N_v and P_{PoS} are small and stable, E_{PoS} is also lower than E_{PoW}, making *PoS* a more sustainable mechanism.

The energy savings can be thus given by Eq. (3.30):

$$E_{savings} = E_{PoW} - E_{PoS} = \int_0^T P_{PoW}(t)dt - \int_0^T N_v \, X \, P_{PoS}.dt \tag{3.31}$$

Example:

Let us consider the following:

- $P_{PoW}(t) = 100e^{0.01t}$ (exponentially increases due to mining difficulty)
- $N_v = 1000$ *validators*
- $P_{PoS} = 1$ *unit of energy per validator*
- $T = 10$ *years*

Using Eq. (3.31)

$$E_{savings} = \int_0^{10} 100e^{0.01t}dt - \int_0^{10} 1000 \text{ X } 1dt = 105,316 - 10,000 = 95,316$$

Thus in 10 years 95,316 units of energy are saved using Proof-of-Stake (*PoS*).

Delegated Proof-of-Stake (*DPoS*)

Another consensus mechanism used nowadays is called *DPoS* (delegated Proof-of-Stake). *DPoS* was initially created by Dan Larimer in 2014, and it's used in numerous blockchains including *EOS, TRON*, and *Steemit*. In *DPoS*, as opposed to all validators or miners who propose and verify blocks, the group of users delegates the obligation to a restricted number of chosen members, called witnesses or delegates, who secure the network and validate transactions.

In *DPoS*, token holders (*token holders are individuals or entities who own number of cryptographic tokens such as cryptocurrency*) cast their votes to pick a group of trustworthy delegates who are liable for verifying transactions and preserving the network. This voting procedure might happen constantly or sporadically.

The voting power of a user V_i is proportional to the number of tokens T_i they hold is given by Eq. (3.32):

$$V_i = k \text{ X } T_i \tag{3.32}$$

where V_i is the voting power of the user i, T_i is the number of tokens staked by user i, and k is a constant that converts the token stake into voting power.

The total votes V_{total} received by a delegate D_j are the sum of votes cast by all voters for that delegate and are shown by Eq. (3.33):

$$V_{total}(D_j) = \sum_{i=1}^{n} V_i(D_j) = \sum_{i=1}^{n} k \text{ X } T_i \tag{3.33}$$

where n is the total number of voters voting for delegate D_j.

The top m delegates (21 or 100, depending on the blockchain) with the highest total votes are selected as active block producers.

Once delegates chosen, they take rounds creating blocks and verifying transactions. This procedure is more swift and energy-efficient than traditional *PoW* systems since fewer nodes (delegates) are certifying the network, decreasing redundancy.

If there are D delegates, each delegate takes turns producing blocks in a round-robin fashion. The number of blocks produced by delegate d can be expressed as in Eq. (3.34):

$$B_d = \frac{B_{total}}{D} \tag{3.34}$$

where B_{total} is the total number of blocks at a given time.

After the delegate satisfactorily validates a block, they earn incentives (typically in the form of new tokens). The delegate often distributes a percentage of these rewards with voters who assisted in selecting them.

If R_d be the total reward earned by delegate d, and r_{voter} be the reward distributed to voters.

If the delegate shares a percentage p of their reward with voters, the reward for the voters is given by Eq. (3.35):

$$r_{voter} = p \ X \ R_d \tag{3.35}$$

And, each voter's share is proportional to their voting power. Thus, the final value of the reward is as shown in Eq. (3.36):

$$r_i = r_{voter} \ X \ V_i \tag{3.36}$$

b) *Interoperability*

Blockchain interoperability implies that multiple blockchain networks may interact and exchange data or assets with one other. This is significant as it enables more *versatility* and *use* of blockchain systems without being restricted to just one blockchain network.

There are four ways of interoperability between blockchains:

1) Cross-chain bridge

A cross-chain bridge permits user to move assets from one blockchain to another by *"locking"* the asset on one blockchain and *"creating"* (minting) the identical asset on another blockchain. This makes certain that the overall value stays the same throughout both blockchains.

Example:

Let us suppose user has 10 tokens on blockchain A and wishes to move them to blockchain B.

This can be shown by Eq. (3.37):

$$f(A_x, B_x) = mint(B_x) \tag{3.37}$$

where A_x is the original 10 tokens on blockchain A that are locked and B_x is an equivalent 10 tokens created (or minted) on blockchain B.

So, user locks 10 tokens on blockchain A, and 10 new tokens appear on blockchain B for use, ensuring that there is no loss of tokens.

2) Atomic swaps

Atomic swaps enable two users exchange tokens across various blockchains without having a central exchange. This ensures that both sides either receive what they desire or nothing happens.

Example:

User A has 5 tokens on blockchain A, and user B has 10 tokens on blockchain B. We are assuming that the value of token in blockchain A is double to that of tokens in blockchain B. The users A and B want to exchange the tokens (which is called as *atomic swaps*) This can be written as shown in Eq. (3.38):

$$Swap\left(A_x, B_y\right) = \begin{cases} Transfer\left(A_x \rightarrow B_y\right), if \ both \ conditions \ are \ met \\ Revert\left(A_x, B_y\right), if \ conditions \ fail \end{cases} \qquad (3.38)$$

A_x: $A's$ token in blockchain A

B_y: $B's$ token in blockchain B

Both A and B lock their tokens in smart contracts, and the swap occurs when both conditions are validated; otherwise the transaction is canceled.

3) Token exchange rate

If a user wishes to transfer tokens from blockchain A to blockchain B, but the value of token varies, then we need to convert the values of tokens, as shown by Eq. (3.39):

$$B_y = A_x \ X \ e_{A \rightarrow B} \qquad (3.39)$$

where A_x is the number of tokens on blockchain A and $e_{A \rightarrow B}$ is the exchange rate of transfer, and B_y is the number of tokens received on blockchain B.

Example:

If one token on blockchain A is equal to two tokens on blockchain B, then $e_{A \rightarrow B}$ is 2. If user x from blockchain A wants to send 10 tokens to user y on blockchain B, then the total number of tokens received is

$$B_y = 10 \ X \ 2 = 20 \ \text{tokens}$$

4) Cross-chain transaction fees

Cross-chain transaction fees refer to the costs related to transferring tokens across different blockchains. This may be expressed by Eq. (3.40):

$$B_y = (A_x \; X \; e_{A \to B}) \; X \; (1 - F_{A \to B}) \tag{3.40}$$

where $F_{A \to B}$ is the cross-chain transaction fees

If one token on blockchain A is equal to two tokens on blockchain B, then $e_{A \to B}$ is 2. Also, the transaction fee is 1%. If user x from blockchain A wants to send 10 tokens to user y on blockchain B, then the total number of tokens received are

$$B_y = (10 \; X \; 2) \; X \; (1 - 0.01) = 19.8 \text{ tokens}$$

c) *Integration with AI*

Blockchain and AI integration combines the features of both technologies to generate systems that are secure and transparent.

1) Data Security and Integrity

Data stored on blockchain ensures that it hasn't been altered. Blockchain helps ensure the authenticity of data when AI requires to use the data for decision-making.

Example:

Let's consider that there is data D stored on the blockchain, and the unique fingerprint for the data is denoted by $hash(D)$. When AI wants to use the data, it checks the $hash(D)$, and if it matches with the hash generated from the data (D), it is authentic; otherwise, it is not.

2) AI-Enhanced Blockchain Consensus

Certain systems in blockchain networks rely on validators to validate transactions. Using historical data, AI can assist in selecting the most effective validators.

The likelihood of choosing a validator (V_i) could depend on an AI-generated score as given by Eq. (3.41):

$$P(V_i) = \frac{Score(V_i)}{\sum\limits_{j=1}^{n} Score(V_j)} \tag{3.41}$$

This implies that a validator's chances of being chosen increase with its performance.

3) Predictions by AI

AI can forecast future events by using historical data. For instance, AI may forecast the following value, d_{n+1}, using the historical data $D = \{d_1, d_2, ..., d_n\}$. Eq. (3.42) denotes the prediction by using AI using the data stored in the blockchain.

$$d_{n+1} = f(D) \tag{3.42}$$

3.6   Ethical Considerations

The use of blockchain for business has ethical considerations, and it's imperative to ensure that these ethical considerations are well addressed. The seven key ethical considerations for businesses using blockchain are:

a) *Privacy and data concerns*

Blockchain is transparent and all transactions are documented on a public ledger that is open to everyone. Although this guarantees culpability and trust, it may result in privacy breaches since transaction-related personal information may become public. Data uploaded to the blockchain cannot be removed or changed once it is published. If private or erroneous data is kept indefinitely, its immutability raises ethical concerns.

b) *Consensus algorithm and environmental impact*

Proof-of-Work (*PoW*) is a consensus technique used by blockchains like Bitcoin and Ethereum (before Ethereum 2.0), which consumes a lot of energy due to its high processing power requirements. This brings up ethical concerns regarding the environmental effects of blockchain. If alternatives that are more sustainable, such as Proof-of-Stake (*PoS*) or delegated Proof-of-Stake (*DPoS*), are used, these should be used in blockchain.

c) *Illegal activities*

The anonymity of blockchain technology makes it possible for illicit operations including tax evasion, money laundering, and terrorist funding. This presents an ethical conundrum to balance between the right to privacy and the necessity of curtailing illegal use. The usage of cryptocurrencies in dark web marketplaces and decentralized platforms could assist with the promoting of illicit goods and services.

d) *Regulatory compliance*

Blockchain technology is global, but its use is governed differently in each nation. It is essential to guarantee adherence to local regulations, including those pertaining to know your customer (KYC) and anti-money laundering (AML), but enforcing them might pose challenges in decentralized systems. By adopting blockchain to operate in countries with permissive rules, some businesses may take advantage of regulatory loopholes, creating ethical dilemmas regarding dodging taxes or labor or environmental standards.

e) *Ethical concerns related to smart contracts*

Blockchain-based smart contracts do not allow for human involvement; instead, they operate automatically when certain criteria are fulfilled. This raises issues of accountability and fairness in the occurrence of unanticipated events. Courts may be used to settle disputes in a conventional legal structure, which is not in case of blockchain technology. Smart contracts make transactions definitive once the requirements are satisfied, which may not always be ethically acceptable if one party loses out as a result of misunderstandings or technological difficulties.

f) *Algorithmic biasness*

Bias in the blockchain algorithms used might result in biased outcomes if AI is included for decision-making or validation. This might show up as discrimination or disparate possibilities in the event that the computational model or underlying data is erroneous.

g) *Tokenization*

Tokenization, the practice of distributing digital tokens, is often used in blockchain. Treating these tokens as investments has the potential to cause financial problems. Pump-and-dump operations, in which the price of a token is artificially boosted and then immediately sold off, are commonplace due to the volatility of cryptocurrency markets and may cause damage to naive participants.

Exercise

Exercise 1

Assume a company. MedicSec is deploying blockchain technology to safely handle patient information across numerous hospitals. Every time a hospital updates a patient's record, a new transaction gets generated. This transaction is put to a block, which is then connected to previous blocks, forming a secured chain of data. The blockchain network comprises numerous nodes (each symbolizing a hospital), which must authenticate each transaction to guarantee the data are correct and uniform throughout the network.

Prepare report based on the following four questions:

(a) Describe the role of blocks and chains in MedicSec's blockchain.
(b) Clarify the relevance of nodes in MedicSec's blockchain network.
(c) Establish the transaction validation procedure in MedicSec's blockchain system.
(d) Demonstrate how the framework of a blockchain assists preserve patient data integrity and security in MedicSec's network.

(The name of the company used in the business scenario is hypothetical and is not intended to represent any actual business)

Exercise 2

ABC Foods, a worldwide food supplier, and HealthiMe, a healthcare provider network, are researching blockchain to strengthen their operations. ABC Foods intends to promote supply chain transparency by tracing the flow from source to plate, ensuring food safety and eliminating waste. HealthiMe wants to employ blockchain to handle patient data securely, giving authenticated access to patient information throughout its network of healthcare providers.

Questions:

1. Identify the major advantages of blockchain for ABC Foods and HealthiMe?
Examine the following aspects of the answer:

- *How does blockchain increase traceability and safety in ABC Foods's supply chain?*
- *How does it boost data security and accessibility for HealthiMe?*

2. Analyze the obstacles ABC Foods and HealthiMe would experience while employing blockchain.
Consider the following point to answer:

- *What are some possible challenges a business could confront, such as regulatory compliance in healthcare or supply chain data accuracy?*

3. Clarify the overlaps as well as variations in how ABC Foods and HealthiMe leverage blockchain.
Reflect the following point to answer:

- *How does each company's blockchain use vary in terms of the kind of data maintained and the goal (supply chain tracking vs. data security)? What commonalities exist: the need for openness and trust?*

4. Assess how blockchain meets specific industry demands for both businesses.
Consider the following point to answer:

- *Why may ABC Foods emphasize real-time monitoring features, whereas HealthiMe focuses on safe, permissioned access to records?*

Exercise 3

Business Scenario 1:

123Bank, a business that provides financial services, is introducing a new regulatory technology (RegTech) platform aimed to lower compliance costs gradually. The first yearly compliance cost for 123Bank is $120,000. The new method is intended to lower these expenditures by 30% over a 5-year period. 123Bank's finance team needs to assess the overall savings from this cost reduction to see whether the new RegTech solution is a reasonable investment. Calculate the overall compliance cost reductions 123GreenBank will accomplish over 5 years utilizing the RegTech solution.

Business Scenario 2:

PayMe, a digital transactions startup, has opted for investing in blockchain technology to expand its services via tokenization, anticipating this leads to more income. With a starting capital of 100,000, the business expects generating 50,000 yearly in additional income via tokenization over the following 5 years. Assuming a discount rate of 5%, PayMe's finance team seeks to determine if this blockchain investment would provide a positive return and contribute long-term value to the the business.

Questions:

Estimate the future value of PayMe's income from the blockchain investment after 5 years, and analyze the net present value (NPV) result.

Exercise 4: Ethical Implications of Blockchain

Objective To explore the ethical considerations of using blockchain technology in business.

Task Discuss the ethical implications of blockchain technology, focusing on privacy, data security, and potential misuse. Provide recommendations for ethical best practices.

Deliverables:
- A report discussing the ethical issues and potential solutions.
- A set of guidelines (one page) for businesses to follow to ensure ethical use of blockchain technology.

References

Alzoubi, Y. I., & Mishra, A. (2023). Green blockchain – A move towards sustainability. *Journal of Cleaner Production, 430*, 139541. https://doi.org/10.1016/j.jclepro.2023.139541

Brittany, W. (2022, March 8). *Ethereum 2.0: Shifting from proof-of-work to proof-of-stake*. Upstate Interactive. https://medium.com/upstate-interactive/ethereum-2-0-677535a400e0

Duan, K., Pang, G., & Lin, Y. (2023). Exploring the current status and future opportunities of blockchain technology adoption and application in supply chain management. *Journal of Digital Economy, 2*, 244–288. https://doi.org/10.1016/j.jdec.2024.01.005

Ducrée, J. (2022). *Satoshi Nakamoto and the Origins of Bitcoin—Narratio in Nomine, Datis et Numeris*. https://doi.org/10.48550/arXiv.2206.10257

Herrera-Joancomartí, J., & Pérez-Solà, C. (2016). *Privacy in bitcoin transactions: New challenges from blockchain scalability solutions. 9880*, 26–44. https://doi.org/10.1007/978-3-319-45656-0_3

Jasim, Z., & Hadi, A. (2023). *Study on blockchain scalability methods limitation and solution* (pp. 220–225). https://doi.org/10.1109/ICESAT58213.2023.10347291

Kwaasteniet, A. d. (2019, September 11). The nonsense of.... TPS (transactions per second). *Medium.* https://medium.com/@aat.de.kwaasteniet/the-nonsense-of-tps-transactions-per-second-2d7156df5e53

Nakamoto, S. (2008). *Bitcoin: A peer-to-peer electronic cash system.*

Sklaroff, J. M. (2017). Smart contracts and the cost of inflexibility. *University of Pennsylvania Law Review, 166*(1), 263–303. https://www.jstor.org/stable/45154933

Vujičić, D., Jagodic, D., & Randić, S. (2018). *Blockchain technology, bitcoin, and Ethereum: A brief overview* (pp. 1–6). https://doi.org/10.1109/INFOTEH.2018.8345547

Chapter 4
Leveraging Cloud Computing

Abstract This chapter covers the benefits of cloud computing and its relevance in current IT infrastructure, concentrating on scalability, cost-efficiency, and accessibility. The first section explains cloud computing foundations and the three primary service models: Infrastructure as a Service (IaaS), Platform as a Service (PaaS), and Software as a Service (SaaS). Three deployment models—public, private, and hybrid clouds—are studied, emphasizing their distinct advantages and applicability for diverse business objectives. The chapter looks into options for cloud migration, such as lift-and-shift, replatforming, and rearchitecting, stressing their financial implications. It also covers the total cost of ownership (TCO) in cloud computing, with a comparison of pricing models such pay-as-you-go, reserved instances, and spot instances. Finally, the chapter explores security and compliance in cloud systems, concentrating on public, private, and hybrid clouds, and describes cost optimization measures such as rightsizing, leveraging discounts, and monitoring usage to increase efficiency and minimize expenditures.

Keywords Scalability · Cost-efficiency · Cloud migration · Total cost of ownership (TCO) · Public cloud · Private cloud · Hybrid cloud · Security and compliance · Pay-as-you-go · Reserved instances · Spot instances · Rightsizing resources · Cloud service models · Cloud deployment models

4.1 Introduction

Cloud computing has come to be the foundation of current IT infrastructure, providing businesses with unparalleled scalability, cost-efficiency, accessibility, and reliability. Understanding the several aspects of cloud computing is critical as businesses transition to cloud-based solutions. This chapter provides a discussion of how businesses could capitalize from cloud computing, covering topics from fundamental concepts and migration strategies to economic consequences and security concerns. Exploring these factors will give businesses a better understanding of how cloud computing benefits business operations.

The first part, Introduction to Cloud Computing, provides a basic introduction of cloud computing. It explores into the fundamental ideas, characteristics, and advantages that define cloud computing. The different service models—Infrastructure as a Service (IaaS), Platform as a Service (PaaS), and Software as a Service (SaaS), as well as the various deployment types, such as public, private, and hybrid clouds, are also discussed.

The second part, Strategies for Migrating to the Cloud, focuses on the actual challenges of cloud migration. This section discusses the essential methods and best practices for migrating current IT infrastructure and applications to the Cloud. The three migration options, lift-and-shift, replatforming, and rearchitecting, are reviewed with perspectives on how businesses may choose the migration strategies.

The third part, Economic Considerations for Choosing Cloud Service Providers and Deployment Models, focuses on the financial consequences of cloud computing. It describes how to calculate the total cost of ownership (TCO) and compare various pricing models, such as pay-as-you-go, reserved instances, and spot instances. This section also looks at the financial implications of various deployment models and suggests cost optimization strategies.

The final section examines cloud security and compliance across three deployment models: public, private, and hybrid clouds. In the public cloud, security is split between the service provider, who guarantees the infrastructure, and the business, which handles data and access control, yet external threats exist. For private clouds, businesses have greater authority but also more responsibility for internal and external risks. In hybrid clouds, security problems emerge around data movement between public and private environments, compliance integration, and identity and access management (IAM). The explanation in the section represents security in various circumstances, illustrating how encryption, secure data transfer protocols, and vulnerability management may minimize risks, while compliance and effective IAM increase security across cloud systems. In hybrid clouds, balancing these aspects improves security.

4.2 Fundamental Concepts of Cloud Computing

Cloud computing is the provision of computer services over the Internet, including servers, storage, databases, networking, software, and applications (Dikaiakos et al., 2009). Businesses may use these resources *on-demand* from a cloud provider instead of owning and maintaining them. Thus, businesses benefits because of the following reasons:

- *On-demand self-service resource allocation:* Businesses can set up and manage their own computing resources without the need to interact with the service provider.
- *Broad network access:* Businesses can use the resources over the Internet through the number of devices such as mobile phones, tablets, and PCs.

- *Resource pooling:* Cloud providers gather resources to serve multiple businesses. The system adjusts the allocation of resources based on the needs of each business.
- *Rapid elasticity:* Resources can be easily and rapidly increased or decreased based on demand, allowing businesses to scale up or down as needed.
- *Measured service:* Cloud services use metering system to track and manage these resources, automatically adjusting usage to optimize performance and efficiency.

Some of the examples where the adoption of cloud services facilitated businesses:

- Coca-Cola uses Amazon online Services (AWS) to control seasonal online traffic surges during campaigns for advertising. Coca-Cola managed increasing demand by changing the server capacity requirements up and down as needed, therefore avoiding the need for long-term infrastructure spending (Amazon Web Services, 2022).
- Netflix uses AWS to flexibly expand to meet changing demand, such as during the premiere of a popular new season. This approach offers flawless streaming experiences (Humbert, 2024).
- Airbnb employs AWS to manage traffic spikes during busy booking seasons. AWS enabled Airbnb to handle rising demand economically (Amazon Web Services, 2019).
- HDFC Bank uses cloud computing to manage all of its large transactions with uninterrupted efficiency and satisfied customers (Sandhya, 2024).
- Emirates Airlines employs Microsoft Azure to manage increases in online traffic. Azure's flexible cloud infrastructure enables Emirates maintain impeccable booking process (Microsoft, 2022).

4.2.1 Features of Cloud Computing

The key features of cloud computing include:

Scalability
Scalability refers to the dynamic allocation of computing resources to businesses, allowing us to adjust resource use in real time (Xiao et al., 2013).

If $R(T)$ represent the resources at any given time T, scalability is given by Eq. 4.1:

$$R(T) = R_0 + \int_0^T \frac{dD(t)}{dt} dt \tag{4.1}$$

where R_0 is the initial resource allocation, $D(t)$ represents the demand at time t, and $\frac{dD(t)}{dt}$ is the rate of change of demand over time.

Thus, Eq. 4.1 illustrates how cloud services automatically perform the dynamic allocation of resources (Armbrust et al., 2010). In traditional infrastructure, businesses often allocate static resources, whereas, in cloud platforms like AWS or Google Cloud, resources scale up or down based on usage.

The demand $D(t)$ grows exponentially over time; thus,

$$D(t) = D_0 * e^{kt} \tag{4.2}$$

where D_0 the initial demand at $t = 0$, and k is the growth rate of demand.

The resource requirements change due to high demand; differentiating Eq. 4.2 gives the rate of change of demand in time t, as mentioned by Eq. 4.3.

$$\frac{dD(t)}{dt} = k * D_0 * e^{kt} \tag{4.3}$$

Placing Eq. 4.3 in 4.1, the resource allocation can be stated in Eq. 4.4.

$$R(T) = R_0 + \int_0^t k * D_0 * e^{kt} dt \tag{4.4}$$

Thus, the scalability of resource allocation is given by Eq. 4.5.

$$R(T) = R_0 + k * D_0 * \left(e^{kt} - 1\right) \tag{4.5}$$

This is the expanded scalability equation, which shows how resources increase over time as demand grows exponentially. In Eq. 4.5, R_0 is the base resources required by businesses and is always allocated regardless of demand, and $D_0 * (e^{kt} - 1)$ captures additional resources that are allocated over time as demand grows.

Cost-Efficiency

Cloud computing uses *pay-as-you-go (PAYG)* mode which includes the fixed cost and cost pertaining to the resources used by business over time (Rajkumar et al., 2010).

The cost can be represented as a function of time, $C(T)$, as mentioned in Eq. 4.6

$$C(T) = C_0 + \int_0^t R(t).P dt \tag{4.6}$$

where C_0 represents fixed costs, $R(t)$ is the resource usage by business over time, and P is the price per unit of resource required.

Equation (4.6) shows that costs are directly proportional to the resources used over time. Also, in Eq. 4.6, the resource usage by businesses $R(t)$ is a variable cost and varies based on demand fluctuations. As in scalability, we know that resource usage grows exponentially over time due to demand; then $R(t)$ can be represented as in Eq. 4.7:

$$R(t) = R_0 * e^{kt} \tag{4.7}$$

where R_0 is the initial resource usage at $t = 0$, and k is the growth rate of resource usage.

Using Eq. (4.7) in (4.6), cost-efficiency equation can be given by Eq. 4.8:

$$\boldsymbol{C(T) = C_0 + \int_0^t R_0 * e^{kt}.Pdt} \tag{4.8}$$

Solving and simplifying Eq. 4.8, we get

$$\boldsymbol{C(T) = C_0 + \frac{R_0 * P}{k} * \left(e^{kt} - 1\right)} \tag{4.9}$$

Equation 4.9 shows that, while the base cost C_0 remains constant, the variable cost, $\frac{R_0*P}{k} * \left(e^{kt} - 1\right)$, grows exponentially over time. The pay-as-you-go model thus ensures that businesses only pay for resources they use.

Accessibility
Cloud computing allows businesses to access the resources and services that can be accessed online (Rimal et al., 2011). The accessibility of cloud resources can be modeled by measuring how many users can access the system online and is expressed by Eq. 4.10:

$$A(T) = \frac{U(t)}{U_{max}} \tag{4.10}$$

where $U(t)$ is the number of active users at any given time t, and U_{max} is the maximum capacity of the system.

If accessibility, $A(T)$, approaches 1, it means nearly all users can access the system at all times. Cloud platforms like Microsoft Azure use load-balancing and distributed architecture to ensure that resources are available to the businesses even under heavy demand (Marinos & Briscoe, 2009).

In an actual scenario, the number of users $U(t)$ fluctuates over time. For simplicity, if we consider that user growth is exponential over time, then $U(t)$ is:

$$U(t) = U_0 * e^{kt} \tag{4.11}$$

where U_0 is the initial number of users at $t = 0$, and k is the growth rate of users over time.

From Eqs. 4.11 and 4.10, we get:

$$A(T) = \frac{U_0 * e^{kt}}{U_{max}} \tag{4.12}$$

Equation 4.12 thus shows how accessibility is influenced by the number of users over time relative to the maximum capacity of the cloud system.

The cloud services by companies like AWS or Google Cloud dynamically scale their capacity to ensure high accessibility. The maximum capacity, U_{max}, can be represented as a function of time as in Eq. 4.13.

$$U_{max}(t) = U_{max}^0 * e^{\lambda t} \tag{4.13}$$

where U_{max}^0 is the initial maximum capacity and λ is the growth rate of system capacity over time.

Substituting Eq. 4.13 in 4.12 and simplifying, we get

$$A(T) = \frac{U_0}{U_{max}^0} * e^{(k-\lambda)t} \tag{4.14}$$

For simplicity, Eq. 4.14 can be further rewritten as:

$$A(T) = A_0 * e^{(k-\lambda)t} \tag{4.15}$$

where $A_0 = \frac{U_0}{U_{max}^0}$ is the initial accessibility at $t = 0$ and $e^{(k-\lambda)t}$ models the growth rate of users compared to the system's capacity. There can be three conditions:

- If $k > \lambda$, user growth outpaces system capacity growth, and accessibility decreases over time.
- If $k < \lambda$, system capacity grows faster than user growth, and accessibility improves over time.
- If $k = \lambda$, accessibility remains constant as the cloud system scales perfectly in line with user demand.

The aim of the cloud service providers is to adjust λ and map with k, which is the ideal situation. In such cases, $A(T) = A_0$, the cloud system grows at exactly the same rate as business demand.

Reliability

Reliability measures the amount of time the cloud systems are working appropriately without any failure (Mesbahi et al., 2018). To measure reliability, $R(t)$, we model the probability that the system will work over a given period, and is represented by Eq. 4.16.

$$R(T) = e^{-\lambda(t)} \tag{4.16}$$

where $\lambda(t)$ is the failure rate at any given time t.

The aim for cloud provider is that cloud systems should have higher uptime. In order to do so, cloud providers use redundant systems, disaster recovery, or automatic failover mechanisms (Zhang et al., 2010).

The failure rate $\lambda(t)$ is not always constant and can be represented as:

$$\lambda(t) = \lambda_0 + \alpha.t \tag{4.17}$$

where λ_0 is the initial failure rate, and α is the rate of change of the failure rate over time.

Putting Eq. 4.17 into 4.16 and evaluating over time t, we get

$$R(T) = e^{-\int_0^t (\lambda_0 + \alpha.t)dt} = e^{-\left(\lambda_0.t + \frac{\alpha t^2}{2}\right)} \tag{4.18}$$

In Eq. 4.18,

- $\lambda_0.t$ represents the constant failure rate λ_0 during the initial phase of the system's operation.
- $\frac{\alpha t^2}{2}$ represents the impact of the changing failure rate α and shows how the system's reliability degrades (or improves) over time.

If $\alpha > 0$, the failure rate increases over time, and if $\alpha < 0$, the failure rate decreases over time (representing improvements in system reliability).

To avoid situations of $\alpha > 0$, cloud systems often incorporate redundancy, meaning that multiple instances of the same services are deployed to provide backup. If a system has n redundant components, the overall system reliability improves.

For a system with n independent, redundant components, each with reliability $R(T)$, the overall reliability $R_{total}(T)$ is given by Eq. 4.19.

$$R_{total}(T) = 1 - (1 - R(T))^n \tag{4.19}$$

In Eq. 4.19, $1 - R(T)$ gives the probability of failure of one component in cloud system, $(1 - R(T))^n$ is the probability of failure of n components, and $1 - (1 - R(T))^n$ gives the probability that at least one component is still working.

Substituting Eq. 4.18 into Eq. 4.19, the total redundancy can be given by Eq. 4.20.

$$R_{total}(T) = 1 - \left(1 - e^{-\left(\lambda_0.t + \frac{\alpha t^2}{2}\right)}\right)^n \tag{4.20}$$

Equation 4.20 indicates that the reliability of cloud services should consider both redundancy and time-varying failure rate for each component in the cloud system.

4.2.2 Service Models of Cloud Computing

Cloud computing provides different types of service models that give businesses with scalable and adaptable IT services. The major service models used by businesses are:

* *Infrastructure as a Service (IaaS)*
* *Platform as a Service (PaaS)*
* *Software as a Service (SaaS)*

IaaS delivers virtualized computing resources (servers, storage, and networking devices) to the businesses online (Manvi & Shyam, 2014). Thus, businesses can access these resources as a service and do not need to spend on actual physical hardware.

PaaS is a platform that allows businesses to build, operate, and maintain software without having to manage the infrastructure (Lawton, 2008).

SaaS provides businesses with the software they need online, eliminating the need for businesses to purchase, install, or maintain software on their own systems, resulting in reduced upfront costs and no maintenance expenses (Benlian & Hess, 2011).

Businesses generally use IaaS or SaaS service models to cut costs and improve operational competence. IaaS provides scalable infrastructure, allowing businesses to outsource computing resources, while SaaS offers software applications online, eradicating the necessity for installation and maintenance (Armbrust et al., 2010; Rajkumar et al., 2010). These cloud models allow businesses to focus on core activities while leveraging flexible, on-demand computing services tailored to their needs (Marston et al., 2011).

Table 4.1 provides details on scalability, cost-efficiency, accessibility, and reliability for different cloud service models, as derived from their equations:

Table 4.1 shows that IaaS demands minimal resource growth and high variable costs, as well as continual accessibility and excellent dependability because of robust backup systems. PaaS has no resource growth, fixed costs, low accessibility, and low reliability, suggesting limited adaptability and performance, whereas SaaS has high

Table 4.1 Comparison of cloud service models

Cloud service model	Scalability (Eq. 4.5)	Cost-efficiency (Eq. 4.9)	Accessibility (Eq. 4.15)	Reliability (Eq. 4.20)
IaaS	$R(T) < 1$ (low resource growth)	$C(T) > 1$ (high variable cost)	$A(T) = 0$ (constant accessibility)	$R_{total}(T) > 1$ (high reliability)
PaaS	$R(T) = 0$ (no resource growth)	$C(T) = 0$ (fixed cost, no usage)	$A(T) < 1$ (low accessibility)	$R_{total}(T) = 0$ (low reliability)
SaaS	$R(T) > 1$ (high resource growth)	$C(T) < 1$ (low variable cost)	$A(T) > 1$ (high accessibility)	$R_{total}(T) < 1$ (moderate reliability)

resource growth, low variable costs, and high accessibility, but moderate reliability, meaning that it scales well and gives outstanding user access.

4.2.3 Cloud Computing Deployment Models

Cloud computing deployment models explain how cloud services are provided by cloud providers for the businesses. The three basic deployment types are:

Public Cloud
Public cloud is a cloud environment where services and infrastructure are hosted and managed by third-party providers (Marozzo, 2019) (e.g., AWS, Google Cloud, Microsoft Azure). These resources are made available to the general public or multiple businesses over the Internet.

Private Cloud
Private cloud is a cloud infrastructure that is exclusively used by a single business (Sotomayor et al., 2009). It can be hosted on-premises or by a third-party provider but is dedicated solely to one business.

Hybrid Cloud
Hybrid cloud is a combination of public and private clouds, allowing data and applications to be shared between them (Toosi et al., 2018). Businesses can store sensitive data in the private cloud and use the public cloud for handling high workloads or non-sensitive operations.

Table 4.2 compares public cloud, private cloud, and hybrid cloud based on scalability, cost-efficiency, accessibility, and reliability:

Table 4.1 shows the variations in how these cloud models handle scalability, cost, accessibility, and reliability, with public cloud giving high scalability and accessibility, private cloud offering high reliability but low scalability, and hybrid cloud establishing a middle ground between the two extremes.

Table 4.2 Comparison of public, private, and hybrid cloud models

Cloud model	Scalability (Eq. 4.5)	Cost-efficiency (Eq. 4.9)	Accessibility (Eq. 4.15)	Reliability (Eq. 4.20)
Public cloud	$R(T) > 1$ (high resource growth)	$C(T) < 1$ (low variable cost)	$A(T) > 1$ (high accessibility)	$R_{total}(T) < 1$ (moderate reliability)
Private cloud	$R(T) = 0$ (no resource growth)	$C(T) = 0$ (fixed cost, no usage)	$A(T) < 1$ (low accessibility)	$R_{total}(T) > 1$ (high reliability)
Hybrid cloud	$R(T) \approx 1$ (balanced resource growth)	$C(T) \approx 1$ (balanced cost)	$A(T) \approx 1$ (moderate accessibility)	$R_{total}(T) \approx 1$ (moderate reliability)

4.3   Strategies for Migrating to the Cloud

Cloud migration includes shifting data, applications, or infrastructure located within the business to the cloud. The migration might occur to public clouds, private clouds, or hybrid clouds. To whatever cloud deployment models businesses decide to shift, there are three options for cloud migration (Li et al., 2023):

- *Lift-and-shift*
- *Replatforming*
- *Rearchitecting*

Each approach has different levels of complexity and costs, which should be examined to assist businesses make sensible decisions.

In this part, we'll analyze the three options and give extensive explanations with reference to cost.

Lift-and-Shift

Lift-and-shift is the easiest migration approach where businesses relocate the current infrastructure to the cloud without doing any modifications in the design. This technique is the fastest and most cost-effective, but it may not fully leverage cloud advantages like scalability and cost reductions.

If $C_{on-premises}$ is the total cost of the on-premises infrastructure,

$C_{cloud}(t)$ is the cost of maintaining resources in the cloud over time t, and

$R(t)$ represents the resources required over time t

Then the total cost of maintaining resources in the lift-and-shift strategy can be mathematically given by Eq. 4.21:

$$C_{cloud}(t) = C_0 + \int_0^t R(t).P_{cloud}dt \qquad (4.21)$$

where C_0 is the initial setup cost,

$R(t)$ is the resource consumption over time t, and

P_{cloud} is the price per unit of cloud resources.

For lift-and-shift migration strategy, the resource usage is constant; thus

$$R(t) = R_0$$

Thus, the total cost over time is

$$C_{cloud}(t) = C_0 + R_0 * P_{cloud} * t \qquad (4.22)$$

The aim of the businesses is $C_{cloud}(t) < C_{on-premises}(t)$.

Replatforming

Replatforming involves making slight adjustments to applications to optimize them for the cloud environment. This approach is more complex than lift-and-shift but offers better cloud optimization.

In replatforming, there are two cost involved:

Initial modification cost C_0, and

recurring cloud costs (also called as modification cost), $C_{modification}$.

Thus, the total cost is given by Eq. (4.23)

$$C_{replatform}(t) = C_0 + C_{modification} + \int_0^t R(t).P_{cloud} dt \qquad (4.23)$$

For replatforming, there is reduced resource consumption due to cloud optimization. If we assume that the resource usage decreases by factor α after optimization, then

$$R(t) = \alpha.R_0$$

where R_0 is the base resource usage (indicating the computing resources before optimization), and $0 < \alpha < 1$ represents the efficiency gained through optimization.

Thus, the final cost for replatforming can be expressed as:

$$C_{replatform}(t) = C_0 + C_{modification} + \int_0^t \alpha.R_0.P_{cloud} dt \qquad (4.24)$$

Rearchitecting

Rearchitecting involves redesigning the entire business applications to be shifted to the cloud. By doing so, the businesses get the advantage of auto-scaling. Though this is the most complex migration strategy, it also provides long-term benefits to businesses in terms of scalability and cost.

Although rearchitecting requires substantial initial development costs, over time expenses may be minimized by making effective use of cloud-native services. Thus, the cost function can be denoted by Eq. (4.25):

$$C_{rearchitect}(t) = C_0 + C_{development} + \int_0^t R(t).P_{cloud} dt \qquad (4.25)$$

where $C_{development}$ represents the development cost for rearchitecting the complete business applications to be moved to cloud.

The biggest advantage of rearchitecting is of auto-scaling, where the resources used by businesses increase or decrease based on demand. If the demand follows the exponential growth of $D(t) = D_0 * e^{kt}$, where k is the demand growth rate, the resource requirement can be denoted by Eq. (4.26):

$$R(T) = R_0 + \int_0^T \frac{dD(t)}{dt} dt = R_0 + D_0\left(e^{kt} - 1\right) \tag{4.26}$$

Substituting Eq. 4.26 in 4.25, we get:

$$C_{rearchitect}(t) = C_0 + C_{development} + \int_0^t \left[R_0 + D_0\left(e^{kt} - 1\right)\right].P_{cloud} dt \tag{4.27}$$

Based on Eq. (4.27), the final cost for replatforming can be expressed as

$$C_{rearchitect}(t) = C_0 + C_{development} + P_{cloud}\left[R_0 t + D_0\left(\frac{e^{kt} - 1}{t}\right)\right] \tag{4.28}$$

In the equation, $R_0 t$ is the base resource usage over time, and $\frac{e^{kt} - 1}{t}$ captures the exponential growth in demand over time.

4.4   Economic Considerations for Choosing Cloud Service Providers and Deployment Models

The financial consequences of cloud computing are a critical decision when selecting cloud service providers and deployment models. At first, we will discuss about the total cost of ownership (TCO) of having cloud resources. Then, we need to understand about various pricing models (*pay-as-you-go, reserved instances, and spot instances*) using TCO and calculate for different types of service providers and deployment models. We will also discuss strategies for cost optimization strategies including resource rightsizing and leveraging cloud provider discounts. By understanding these economic factors, businesses can make decisions of aligning with their operational needs and requirements.

4.4.1   Total Cost of Ownership

The total cost of ownership (TCO) in cloud computing refers to the overall expenditures spent over time while running applications in the cloud. It comprises both initial (migration, setup) and recurring expenditures (resource utilization, data transfer, and storage).

The TCO equation can be given as the sum of initial setup costs and resource consumption over time

Table 4.3 Comparison of cloud pricing models: pay-as-you-go, reserved instances, and spot instances

Pricing model	Cost	Flexibility	Use case
Pay-as-you-go	Higher in the long term if used continuously	Most flexible—scale resources up or down as needed	Ideal for unpredictable workloads or short-term projects
Reserved instances	Lower cost for long-term usage (up to 75% off)	Less flexible—you commit to a specific amount of resources	Best for steady-state, predictable workloads where resource needs are well understood
Spot instances	Extremely low (up to 90% discount).	Least flexible—can be stopped or terminated at any time by the provider	Best for non-critical workloads

Table 4.4 Comparison of pricing models for public, private, and hybrid clouds

Cloud type	Pay-as-you-go	Reserved instances	Spot instances
Public cloud	Pay for what you use	Lower cost for long-term use	Cheapest, but less reliable
Private cloud	Not typically used	Efficient for long-term use	Not applicable
Hybrid cloud	Scale to public for peaks	Mix of reserved and private	Use for non-critical tasks

Cost Optimization Strategies

Cost optimization strategies using the TCO provide a comprehensive way to account for the total costs over time, including compute, storage, and network resources. The three cost optimization techniques (rightsizing, leveraging discounts, and monitoring usage) can be used to reduce either the resource usage $R(t)$ or the cost per unit P, ultimately lowering the total cost of ownership.

Rightsizing Resources

Businesses may reduce their TCO over time by lowering the values of $R_{compute}(t)$, $R_{storage}(t)$, $R_{network}(t)$ via rightsizing. This involves using primarily the required amount of processing power, storage space, and network bandwidth to avoid over-provisioning. For example, identify underused servers and scale them down to minimize $R_{compute}(t)$, hence lowering the total cost of compute resources.

Leveraging Discounts

Leveraging discounts has an impact on $P_{compute}$, $P_{storage}$, $P_{network}$, which are the unit pricing for each resource. Businesses might reduce their overall costs by subscribing to reserved instances or spot pricing. For example, moving to reserved pricing models for computing resources will reduce $P_{compute}$, lowering compute expenses.

Monitoring Usage

Continuous monitoring of $R_{compute}(t)$, $R_{storage}(t)$, and $R_{network}(t)$ enables businesses to identify spikes, inefficiencies, and underutilization. This helps in the efficient allocation of resources and the proper scaling of consumption. Regularly

Table 4.5 Cost optimization strategies

Cost optimization strategy	Description	How it reduces costs	Challenges	Examples
Rightsizing resources	Adjusting resources to match workload requirements of businesses	Reduces unnecessary over-provisioning by scaling resources (compute, storage, and network) to optimal levels	Requires accurate workload forecasting and continuous analysis	Identifying underutilized servers and scaling down, switching to smaller instance types
Leveraging discounts	Taking advantage of pricing offers from cloud providers, such as reserved instances or spot pricing	Lowers the per-unit cost of resources (compute, storage, network) by committing to long-term use or flexible scheduling	May require upfront commitments and isn't suited for fluctuating workloads	Using reserved instances for predictable workloads, spot instances for non-critical tasks
Monitoring usage	Continuously tracking resource consumption to detect inefficiencies or unnecessary expenses	Enables real-time adjustments to avoid unexpected spikes or over-provisioning; helps identify cost-saving opportunities	Requires robust monitoring tools and the ability to act quickly on insights	Tracking storage that hasn't been accessed and shifting it to cheaper cold storage

monitoring may indicate that some storage resources are seldom used, forcing a transition to lower-cost cold storage, lowering $P_{storage}$, and optimizing overall TCO.

Table 4.5 gives the comparative analysis between three types of cost optimization strategies.

4.5   Cloud Security and Compliance

Security and compliance are an important factor that needs to be considered for cloud computing across different deployment models. The security and compliance of each type of deployment models are different, and the section aims to conceptualize how differently security aspects are dealt with cloud deployment models.

4.5.1   Security and Compliance in Public Cloud

In public cloud, the services are offered online and are shared between multiple businesses. The security issues can be data leakage, unauthorized access, and lack of control over data.

If S_{public} is the overall security in public cloud,
$R_{provider}$ is the security provider by the cloud service provider,
$R_{customer}$ is the security managed by business, and
T is the total security threats, then the security in the public cloud using shared responsibility model can be expressed by Eq. 4.34

$$S_{public} = R_{provider} + R_{customer} - T \qquad (4.34)$$

As can be seen from Eq. (4.34), in public cloud, the businesses have limited control over the physical infrastructure and thus $R_{provider}$ handles most of the infrastructure-level security, whereas businesses are responsible for securing their data and access control and thus $R_{customer}$ manages data and application security.

4.5.2 Security and Compliance in Private Cloud

In private cloud, the services are exclusively used by one business and thus offer greater control over data security. This places more responsibility on the business to secure its infrastructure.

If $S_{private}$ is the overall security in private cloud,
$M_{internal}$ is the security managed internally by the business, and $M_{external}$ is the external threat from outside the business, then the security in the private cloud can thus be given by Eq. 4.35

$$S_{private} = M_{internal} - M_{external} \qquad (4.35)$$

As mentioned in Eq. 4.35, security is managed by the business but has greater threats externally. Thus, it is the responsibility of businesses to minimize these external threats.

4.5.3 Security and Compliance in Hybrid Cloud

In the hybrid cloud model, data and applications are shared between private and public clouds. Thus, the core risk of hybrid cloud is data transfer security, compliance integration, and identity management (IAM).

If S_{hybrid} is the overall security in hybrid cloud, $S_{private}$ is the security in private cloud part of hybrid cloud, S_{public} is the security in public cloud part of hybrid cloud, and $C_{transfer}$ is the risks and compliance issues related to transferring data between private and public cloud, then the security in the hybrid cloud can be expressed using Eq. 4.36

$$S_{hybrid} = \alpha.S_{private} + \beta.S_{public} - C_{transfer} \tag{4.36}$$

where α and β are the weights of the private and public cloud, respectively.

Using Eq. 4.36, let us address the three types of risks in hybrid cloud:

Data Transfer Security

Data transfer Security is captured in the term $C_{transfer}$. To further elaborate, $C_{transfer}$ is a function of:

- Encryption strength (E): How sound the data is encrypted during transfer.
- Transfer protocols (T): Security of the network protocols used (e.g., HTTPS, VPN).
- Vulnerabilities (V): The likelihood of exploits during the data transfer.

We can thus represent data transfer security by Eq. (4.37)

$$C_{transfer} = f(E, T, V) \tag{4.37}$$

where higher encryption and secure transfer protocols reduce the transfer risks, and higher vulnerabilities increase the risks.

Compliance Integration Across Clouds

Compliance integration deals with confirming that both public and private cloud environments adhere to regulatory and policy standards. The compliance for private and public cloud can be mentioned as $C_{private}$ and C_{public}.

Thus, overall compliance can be given as the sum of compliances for private and public clouds, as mentioned by Eq. (4.38)

$$S_{private} = f(C_{private}) \text{ and } S_{public} = f(C_{public}) \tag{4.38}$$

Better compliance integration increases the individual security of the clouds, so higher $C_{private}$ and C_{public} values improve $S_{private}$ and S_{public}, respectively.

Identity and Access Management (IAM)

IAM refers to handling access to resources securely across both cloud environments. IAM plays a critical role in both public and private cloud security and should be part of security for both cloud environments. If $IAM_{private}$ and IAM_{public} are the IAM system in the private and public cloud, respectively, then Eq. (4.39) gives the security of IAM systems

$$S_{private} = f(IAM_{private}) \text{ and } S_{public} = f(IAM_{public}) \tag{4.39}$$

Based on Eqs. (4.37), (4.38), and (4.39) and substituting in Eq. (4.36), we get the final equation for security and compliance for hybrid model:

$$S_{hybrid} = \alpha.f\left(C_{private}, IAM_{private}\right) + \beta.\left(C_{public}, IAM_{public}\right) - f(E, T, V) \qquad (4.40)$$

Based on Eq. (4.40), $\alpha.\ f(C_{private}, IAM_{private})$ is the security of the private cloud based on its compliance level and IAM effectiveness, $\beta.\ (C_{public}, IAM_{public})$ is the security of the public cloud based on its compliance level and IAM effectiveness, and $f(E, T, V)$ defines the risks related to data transfer security.

Thus, we observe that for hybrid cloud by optimizing compliance integration and IAM and minimizing data transfer vulnerabilities, hybrid cloud security gets improved.

Exercises

Exercise 1: Emirates NBD's Cloud Transformation

Emirates NBD, one of the UAE's leading bank, is to update its IT infrastructure to accommodate its expanding digital banking offerings. With an emphasis on providing seamless customer service via mobile and online banking, the bank confronts issues in handling seasonal increases in user traffic, particularly during major promotions. To solve these challenges, Emirates NBD has implemented a hybrid cloud approach that includes both Microsoft Azure for public cloud services and a private cloud for confidential customer information. The bank utilizes Azure Infrastructure as an operation (IaaS) to dynamically expand its computing capabilities, ensuring consistent operation during high demand times while avoiding the need to maintain physical servers. Additionally, Platform as a Service (PaaS) is used to create and manage their in-house applications and the implementation of new digital services. Finally, SaaS platforms such as Microsoft 365 improve cooperation and productivity among the bank's remote workforce. The hybrid architecture provides regulatory compliance while enabling the bank to grow quickly and offer high availability to its customers (Haleem et al., 2022).

Task: How does Emirates NBD's adoption of a hybrid cloud strategy, utilizing both public cloud services like Microsoft Azure and a private cloud for sensitive data, enhance its ability to scale operations during peak traffic periods while ensuring compliance with regulatory standards?

Exercise 2: Cloud Service Models

Infosys Cloud Service Models

Infosys, a global player in consulting and technology services headquartered in India, has effectively used an array of cloud service models—IaaS, PaaS, and SaaS—to improve service delivery and operational effectiveness. Infosys employs Google Cloud Platform (GCP) to offer scalable and flexible computing resources that enable them to handle large-scale data processing and storage demands for customers in sectors such as banking and retail. In terms of Platform as a Service (PaaS), Infosys uses Oracle Cloud PaaS to create customized business apps, providing its customers with superior data analytics, AI, and machine learning capabilities while eliminating the requirement to administer infrastructure. Infosys employs Salesforce as a Software as a support (SaaS) platform to manage customer interactions and improve customer operations, allowing for seamless integration of marketing, sales, and support activities.

These cloud service models have allowed Infosys to cut operating expenses, expand more effectively, and increase the agility of its customer offerings. IaaS provides flexibility and scalability for infrastructure demands, PaaS is a platform for creating and deploying applications, and SaaS provides ready-to-use software solutions to improve business activities.

Deliverables:
1. Case Study Analysis showing how Infosys utilizes IaaS, PaaS, and SaaS in different scenarios.
2. Comparison Report outlining the benefits of each model for Infosys.

Exercise 3: Total Cost of Ownership (TCO)

ABC delivers real-time analytics to customers, needing computation, storage, and network resources. They seek to function constantly for a year (12 months) and require a total setup cost of 5000 for first migration and implementation. ABC needs:

- Computation resources at 100 units each month
- Storage resources at 200 units each month
- Network resources at 50 units per month

The cloud provider provides the following cost per unit for each resource type under various pricing models:

- Pay-As-You-Go: 0.10 (compute), 0.05 (storage), 0.02 (network)
- Reserved instances: 0.07 (compute), 0.04 (storage), 0.015 (network)
- Spot instances: 0.03 (compute), 0.02 (storage), 0.01 (network)

Compute the TCO for each model (PAYG, reserved, and spot) over 12 months and then evaluate the results to identify the most cost-effective alternative for ABC.

Exercise 4: Cloud Security Assessment

ABC Systems maintains its sensitive data in a private cloud but relies on a public cloud for the app's front end. The hybrid cloud architecture enables ABC Systems to match high-security needs for data storage with the versatility of a public cloud for managing customer interactions.

The information collected by ABC Systems is

Private Cloud Security ($S_{private}$)
1. Internal security managed by ABC Systems, $M_{internal} = 80$
2. External threats, $M_{external} = 30$

Using Eq. (4.35), we get $S_{private} = M_{internal} - M_{external}$

Public Cloud Security (S_{public})
1. Security managed by cloud provider, $R_{provider} = 70$
2. Security managed by ABC systems, $R_{customer} = 40$
3. Total security threats, $T = 50$

Using Eq. (4.34), we get $S_{public} = R_{provider} + R_{customer} - T$

Hybrid Cloud Security (S_{hybrid})
1. The hybrid cloud weights for private and public clouds are given as $\alpha = 0.6$ (private cloud weight) and $\beta = 0.4$ (public cloud weight).
2. Transfer risks, $C_{transfer}$, depends on:

   (a) *Encryption Strength (E)* : 85 (higher value indicates stronger encryption)
   (b) *Transfer Protocol Security (T)* : 75
   (c) *Vulnerabilities (V)* : 20

Transfer risk function: $C_{transfer} = f(E, T, V) = E + T - V$
Using Eq. (4.40) for hybrid cloud security:

$$S_{hybrid} = \alpha \cdot S_{private} + \beta \cdot S_{public} - C_{transfer}$$

You are required to prepare the cloud security assessment report.
Hint:
The security breakdown for ABC Systems hybrid cloud model (after calculation, as mentioned in the scenario)

- Private cloud security ($S_{private}$): 50
- Public cloud security (S_{public}): 60
- Data transfer security risks ($C_{transfer}$): 140
- Hybrid cloud security (S_{hybrid}): -86

Analysis The negative result for S_{hybrid} shows that transfer security concerns considerably impair the overall security in the hybrid environment. To counteract this, ABC systems might consider strengthening encryption, employing more secure transmission methods, or limiting vulnerabilities.

References

Amazon Web Services. (2019). *Airbnb scales infrastructure automatically using AWS*. Amazon Web Services. https://aws.amazon.com/solutions/case-studies/airbnb-case-study/

Amazon Web Services. (2022). *The Coca-Cola company on AWS: Case studies, videos, innovator stories*. Amazon Web Services. https://aws.amazon.com/solutions/case-studies/innovators/coca-cola/

Armbrust, M., Fox, A., Griffith, R., Joseph, A. D., Katz, R., Konwinski, A., Lee, G., Patterson, D., Rabkin, A., Stoica, I., & Zaharia, M. (2010). A view of cloud computing. *Communications of the ACM, 53*(4), 50–58. https://doi.org/10.1145/1721654.1721672

Benlian, A., & Hess, T. (2011). Opportunities and risks of software-as-a-service: Findings from a survey of IT executives. *Decision Support Systems, 52*(1), 232–246. https://doi.org/10.1016/j.dss.2011.07.007

Dikaiakos, M. D., Katsaros, D., Mehra, P., Pallis, G., & Vakali, A. (2009). Cloud computing: Distributed internet computing for IT and scientific research. *IEEE Internet Computing, 13*(5), 10–13. https://doi.org/10.1109/MIC.2009.103

Haleem, A., Javaid, M., Qadri, M. A., Singh, R. P., & Suman, R. (2022). Artificial intelligence (AI) applications for marketing: A literature-based study. *International Journal of Intelligent Networks, 3*, 119–132. https://doi.org/10.1016/j.ijin.2022.08.005

Humbert, H. (2024). How Netflix leverages cloud computing for success. *Medium*. https://medium.com/@hugo-humbert/case-study-how-netflix-leverages-cloud-computing-for-success-6964283e1b6e

Lawton, G. (2008). Developing software online with platform-as-a-service technology. *Computer, 41*(6), 13–15. https://doi.org/10.1109/MC.2008.185

Li, S., Liu, H., Li, W., & Sun, W. (2023). An optimization framework for migrating and deploying multiclass enterprise applications into the cloud. *IEEE Transactions on Services Computing, 16*(2), 941–956. https://doi.org/10.1109/TSC.2022.3174216

Manvi, S. S., & Shyam, G. K. (2014). Resource management for Infrastructure as a Service (IaaS) in cloud computing: A survey. *Journal of Network and Computer Applications, 41*, 424–440. https://doi.org/10.1016/j.jnca.2013.10.004

Marinos, A., & Briscoe, G. (2009). Community cloud computing. In M. G. Jaatun, G. Zhao, & C. Rong (Eds.), *Cloud computing* (pp. 472–484). Springer. https://doi.org/10.1007/978-3-642-10665-1_43

Marozzo, F. (2019). *Infrastructures for high-performance computing: Cloud infrastructures* (pp. 240–246). https://doi.org/10.1016/B978-0-12-809633-8.20374-9

Marston, S., Li, Z., Bandyopadhyay, S., Zhang, J., & Ghalsasi, A. (2011). Cloud computing—The business perspective. *Decision Support Systems, 51*(1), 176–189. https://doi.org/10.1016/j.dss.2010.12.006

Mesbahi, M. R., Rahmani, A. M., & Hosseinzadeh, M. (2018). Reliability and high availability in cloud computing environments: A reference roadmap. *Human-Centric Computing and Information Sciences, 8*(1), 20. https://doi.org/10.1186/s13673-018-0143-8

Microsoft. (2022). *Emirates Group creates digital, accessible workplace for employees*. Microsoft Customers Stories. https://ms-f1-sites-03-ea.azurewebsites.net/en-us/story/1429066738321808673-emirates-group-en-united-arab-emirates

Rajkumar, B., James, B., & Andrzej, M. G. (2010). *Cloud computing: Principles and paradigms | Wiley*. Wiley.Com. https://www.wiley.com/en-us/Cloud+Computing%3A+Principles+and+Paradigms-p-9781118002209

Rimal, B. P., Jukan, A., Katsaros, D., & Goeleven, Y. (2011). Architectural requirements for cloud computing systems: An enterprise cloud approach. *Journal of Grid Computing, 9*(1), 3–26. https://doi.org/10.1007/s10723-010-9171-y

Sandhya, M. (2024). *How cloud tech boosts transaction volumes for HDFC securities*. https://www.cio.inc/how-cloud-tech-boosts-transaction-volumes-for-hdfc-securities-a-24621

Sotomayor, B., Montero, R. S., Llorente, I. M., & Foster, I. (2009). Virtual infrastructure management in private and hybrid clouds. *IEEE Internet Computing, 13*(5), 14–22. https://doi.org/10.1109/MIC.2009.119

Toosi, A. N., Sinnott, R. O., & Buyya, R. (2018). Resource provisioning for data-intensive applications with deadline constraints on hybrid clouds using Aneka. *Future Generation Computer Systems, 79*, 765–775. https://doi.org/10.1016/j.future.2017.05.042

Xiao, Z., Song, W., & Chen, Q. (2013). Dynamic resource allocation using virtual machines for cloud computing environment. *IEEE Transactions on Parallel and Distributed Systems, 24*(6), 1107–1117. https://doi.org/10.1109/TPDS.2012.283

Zhang, Q., Cheng, L., & Boutaba, R. (2010). Cloud computing: State-of-the-art and research challenges. *Journal of Internet Services and Applications, 1*(1), 7–18. https://doi.org/10.1007/s13174-010-0007-6

Chapter 5
Data Analytics for Business

Abstract This chapter presents an in-depth analysis of data analytics methodologies employed in business, highlighting both structured and unstructured data. For structured data, the chapter discusses about predictive analytics and explores its function in strengthening business decision-making. Techniques for structured data analytics are examined using supervised learning approaches (e.g., regression and classification models) and unsupervised learning methods (e.g., clustering and dimensionality reduction). Unstructured data analytics, on the other hand, is addressed with an emphasis on sentiment analysis and image analytics, which enable businesses to extract valuable insights from text, images, and other non-tabular data. The Orange data mining tool is used as a tool, showing all the predictive models for businesses.

Keywords Structured data · Unstructured data · Predictive analytics · Supervised learning · Unsupervised learning · Orange data mining · Random Forest · k-Means clustering · Naïve Bayes · PCA · Sentiment analysis · Image analytics

5.1 Introduction

Businesses use data analytics to examine massive amounts of data and find patterns and trends that are relevant. The results of the data analysis provide useful information that aids in the decision-making process for businesses. Today, businesses are using data analytics to maximize the value of data and transform raw information into valuable information.

Data analytics choices help businesses discover how consumers behave, comprehend market patterns, and draw insights from past data, all the while reducing dependence on managers' judgments.

There are several benefits of employing data analytics for businesses, some of those as mentioned below:

Competitive Advantage

Data analytics assists businesses to understand consumer preferences and market trends. By doing so, businesses might surpass the competition and obtain competitive advantages. Ola in India relies on data analytics to improve its ride allocation system by evaluating traffic patterns and consumer trip preferences. Alibaba, the e-commerce business from China, applies data analytics to obtain insights on consumer preferences and deliver tailored recommendations.

Operational Efficiency
Data analytics plays an essential part in improving operations efficiency, by finding any inefficiency, minimizing waste, and improving overall output. Reliance Jio leverages data analytics to analyze consumer usage trends and consequently change network capacity. Amazon uses data analytics for its warehouse operations by analyzing the product demand and storing the items in the warehouses which are near to its store, hence saving handling time. BMW applies data analytics for their production process by foreseeing future breakdowns and scheduling repairs ahead. Dubai International Airport implemented data analytics to determine the passenger flow at the airport and subsequently arranged the security checkpoints, minimizing waiting time and offering better travel experience for the passengers.

Decision-Making
Data analytics helps businesses to evaluate the previous data and anticipate future events. By doing so, the businesses lessen the uncertainty in strategic endeavors. Netflix relies on data analytics to analyze the consumer preferences based on the viewing history and makes decision-making on content acquisition strategy.

Personalized Consumer Experience
Data analytics lets businesses personalize their products, offerings, and marketing tactics to specific consumers. By studying historical consumer behavior, interests, and relationships, businesses may give tailored suggestions and incentives that connect with consumers, ultimately maximizing the consumer experience. Starbucks employs data analytics to provide targeted promotions via its mobile app. By leveraging customer data, including purchase history and location, Starbucks delivers highly targeted offers that perfectly align with consumer interests, significantly boosting customer retention and loyalty.

Fraud Detection
Data analytics plays a significant part in detecting fraudulent activity by examining data trends and oddities. Businesses may proactively handle financial fraud and business interruptions. For example, JPMorgan Chase employs data analytics to monitor transactions in real time to identify probable fraud. Spotting anomalous transaction trends helps JPMorgan to respond early to prevent fraudulent actions. Similarly, PayPal uses data analytics to avoid fraud by examining consumer habits and transaction trends. This helps PayPal to recognize and cease dubious activity before they escalate to serious fraud.

Thus, data analytics is a transforming tool that enables businesses to capitalize on the potential of their data. By turning raw data into useful information, businesses can make informed decisions by predicting future trends and minimizing risk. As more businesses accept data-driven strategies, those that deploy data analytics efficiently will not only survive but expand in the competition.

5.2 Importance of Data Analytics

Data analytics is the process to evaluate huge datasets to identify relations, trends, and observations that enable businesses to make decisions. In today's data-driven corporate market, it has grown into an essential resource for businesses to remain competitive, improve their operations, and boost decision-making processes.

Figure 5.1 displays several forms of data analytics used for examining either structured and unstructured data. From Fig. 5.1, it is obvious that data analytics comprises four distinct types: descriptive, diagnostic, predictive, and prescriptive analytics. By translating the raw data into significant information, data analytics allows businesses to execute data-driven actions, analyze the consumer behavior, and strengthen operational efficiency.

Figure 5.1 depicts how four kinds of data analytics are employed by businesses.

Descriptive Analytics
By condensing historical data, descriptive analytics helps us comprehend what occurred in the past (Aydiner et al., 2019). Descriptive analytics makes use of data mining and aggregation methods to reveal trends, patterns, and outcomes.

Diagnostic Analytics
Diagnostic analytics is the process of exploring deeper into the data to find cause-and-effect relationships and to comprehend why it has happened. Usually based on descriptive analytics, diagnostic analytics assists businesses in understanding the causes of particular patterns (Guo & Li, 2022).

Predictive Analytics
Predictive analytics makes predictions about future events by using historical data (Smith & McConnell, 2024). As predictive analytics uses machine learning and statistical methods to foresee patterns, this helps businesses to action beforehand.

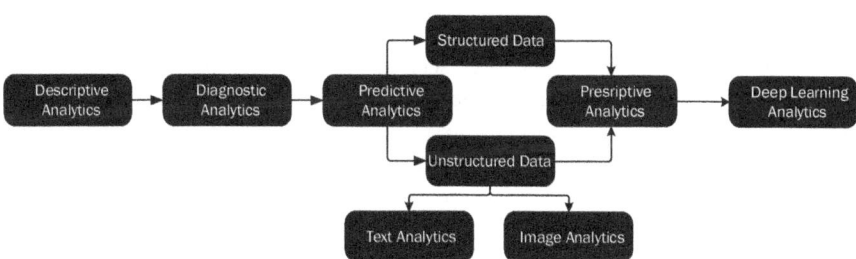

Fig. 5.1 Types of data analytics

Prescriptive Analytics
The predictive analytics provides actions based on the outcomes of the predictive analytics (Wissuchek & Zschech, 2024). The prescriptive analytics considers the effects of different decisions and then helps optimize the action.

This chapter focuses on predictive analytics, the most prevalent data analytics (Wolniak & Grebski, 2023). Predictive analytics works on both structured (where the data is organized into fixed format) and unstructured data (where data is not in fixed format, such as images and videos), and the objective of this chapter is to touch on the essential algorithms used by businesses. Later, the economic feasibility of these algorithms is also discussed in Sect. 5.3.

5.3   Techniques of Data Analytics for Business

In this section of the chapter, we will look in depth at the methodologies applied to predictive analytics in business. To describe the various approaches used, we will emphasize on both supervised and unsupervised learning, with the *Orange data mining tool* providing a practical framework for illustration.

5.3.1   Orange Data Mining Tool

Orange is a data analytics platform with a GUI-based workflow; consequently we don't need to know how to code to use the Orange tool. The tool seamlessly integrates supervised and unsupervised predictive analytics. Orange data mining tool is used efficiently by novices as well as professionals, and is the popular open-source machine learning tool (PredictiveAnalyticsToday, 2024), having a user-friendly graphical interface (as shown in Fig. 5.2).

Setting up the Orange tool
Step 1: Navigate to https://orangedatamining.com/download/ and choose Download.
   (The screenshot is shown in Fig. 5.3.)

Step 2: Once Orange data mining is installed, the platform looks as seen in Fig. 5.4.

The orange starting page appears as seen in Fig. 5.4. The tools on the left-hand side are referred to as filters, and widgets are found inside filters. Widgets serve as the tool's foundation for performing its tasks. We connect widgets and establish workflows, which are the actions we take to execute data analytics.

Fig. 5.2   Free data mining software (PredictiveAnalyticsToday, 2024)

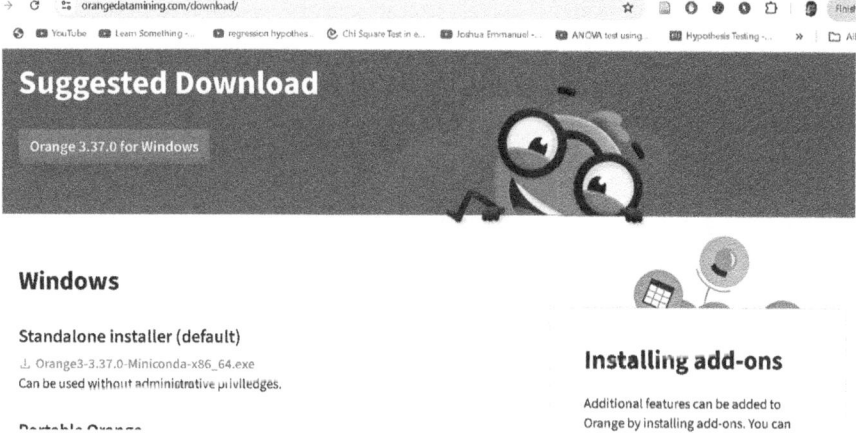

Fig. 5.3   Download page of Orange data mining tool (Source: orangedatamining.com)

5.3.2   Data Analytics Using Structured Data

Data in structured data is kept in a predetermined manner, such as rows and columns in databases or spreadsheets, and is highly ordered and searchable. Structured data is extensively used in businesses for data analytics to support decision-making. For the analysis of structured data, two main categories are often deployed: supervised and unsupervised learning.

Supervised Learning
Supervised learning is one of the main concepts in data analytics. It is a type of data analytics where the algorithm trains from labeled training data to generate

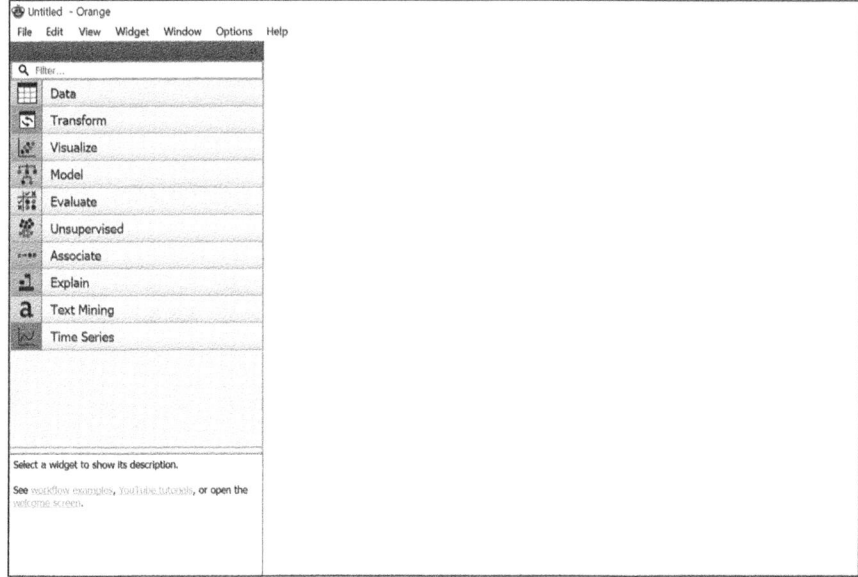

Fig. 5.4 Orange data mining software (Source: orangedatamining.com)

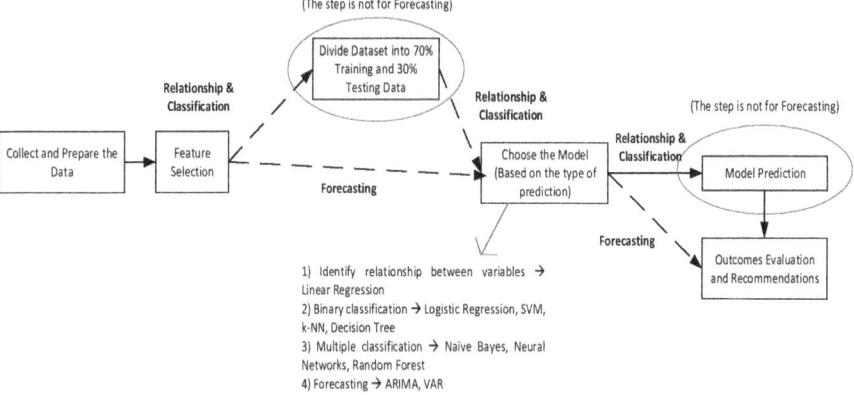

Fig. 5.5 Steps of supervised learning (Source: Self)

predictions without any human intervention. In supervised learning, the algorithm is presented with input–output pairs (examples) and learns to map the input to the matching output. The processes for implementing the supervised learning algorithms may be better illustrated using Fig. 5.5:

The steps for all the supervised algorithms are as follows:

Step 1: Collect and Prepare Data

The business gathers dataset that includes variables to be used for predictions.

Step 2: Feature Selection

The business needs to identify the input variables and classify them into independent and dependent variables. Dependent variable is used by the model to make predictions based on independent variables. We are required to construct conceptual framework as well for predictions.

Step 3: Dataset Division

Divide the dataset into two parts: training data and testing data. The normal practice is 70%–30% or 60%–40%, where 70%/60% training data is used to teach the model, and the 30%/40% testing data is used to evaluate its performance.

Step 4: Choose a Model

Select a type of model to be used based on the type of predictions required. As mentioned in Fig. 5.5, there are the following criteria for model selection:

1. *If we are required to identify relationship between variables → Linear Regression*
2. *Binary classification → Logistic Regression, SVM, k-NN, Decision Tree*
3. *Multiple classification → Naïve Bayes, Neural Networks, Random Forest*
4. *Forecasting → ARIMA*

Step 5: Selection of Model

In the selection of model, the model is trained using the test data and evaluated using the model's accuracy, precision, recall, or other relevant metrics depending on the nature of the problem (e.g., classification, regression).

Step 6: Make Predictions

Once satisfied with the model's performance, the business can use it to make predictions on new and unseen data.

Supervised learning is often used for regression (e.g., stock market price prediction, house price prediction) and classification (e.g., spam email detection). In supervised learning, the model is trained using labeled data, and the aim is to predict the outcomes.

The popular supervised machine learning algorithms are as follows:

1. *Linear Regression:* Linear regression is used for predicting a continuous output variable (also called the dependent variable) based on one or more input features (independent variables) by fitting a linear equation to the data.
2. *Binary classification*

   Logistic Regression: Logistic regression is used for binary classification problems, where the output is a probability value between 0 and 1.

   Support Vector Machines (SVM): SVM is the classification that can be used for both classification and regression. It finds a hyperplane that best separates data points into different classes while maximizing the margin between the classes.

Decision Trees: Decision tree is also used for both classification and regression tasks. It partitions the data into subsets based on the input features, with each partition represented by a tree branch, and each leaf node providing a prediction.
3. *Multiple Classification*

Naive Bayes: Naive Bayes is a multiple classification algorithm based on Bayes' theorem. It is particularly useful for text classification and spam filtering.

Random Forest: Random Forest combines multiple decision trees for more accuracy and is used for both classification and regression tasks.

We will focus on each of them using hypothetical data and Orange data mining tool.

Linear Regression
Regression analysis is a basic statistical tool for examining the relationship between variables and making predictions based on it. It is critical in determining how one or more independent factors influence a dependent variable.

There are two fundamental approaches of linear regression:

1. *Simple linear regression*
2. *Multiple linear regression*

Simple linear regression: This approach considers the relationship between two variables—a single independent variable and a dependent variable.

Multiple linear regression: Multiple linear regression considers the relationship between multiple independent variables and its impact on the dependent variable.

Simple Linear Regression
The equation for simple linear regression is a mathematical representation that relates two variables: a dependent variable, Y, and an independent variable, X. The equation takes the form, as given by Eq. (5.1):

$$Y = aX + b \tag{5.1}$$

In the equation, Y represents the dependent variable that we want to predict, X is the independent variable, and a is the slope of the regression line. The equation represents how much Y is expected to change for a one-unit change in X. If a is positive, it indicates a positive correlation, while if a is negative, it indicates a negative correlation. The b is the intercept of the regression line. It represents the value of Y when X is equal to 0. The goal of simple linear regression is to find the values of a and b that best fit the data.

There are two results that are used to analyze the data:

Result 1:
The values of coefficient a
The value of a helps to quantify the relationship between the independent variable (s) and the dependent variable. This indicates the strength and direction of this relationship.

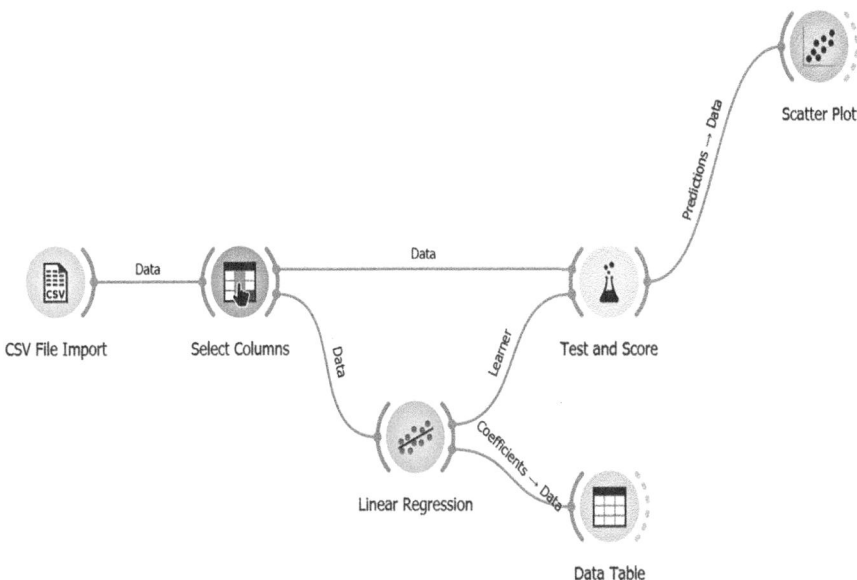

Fig. 5.6 Orange data mining workflow for simple linear regression

Result 2:
The value of R^2

R^2, also known as the coefficient of determination, is a statistical measure used to assess the goodness of fit of a linear regression model.

In most practical cases, R^2 falls between 0 and 1, with higher values being desirable. A higher R^2 suggests that the model is better at explaining and predicting the dependent variable.

The R^2 value is typically a number between 0 and 1, where:

- $R^2 = 0$: This means that the independent variable(s) do not explain any of the variance in the dependent variable.
- $R^2 = 1$: This indicates that the independent variable(s) perfectly explain the variance in the dependent variable.

The workflow for the Simple Linear Regression is given in Fig. 5.6:

Example 5.1:
Imagine you are an HR manager of the company and you are looking to understand and improve employee productivity based on the training hours. To do this, you have collected data from 30 employees over the past year.

Thus, the equation becomes

$$Productivity\ Score = a.(Training\ Hours) + b$$

The format of the dataset is given as under:

Training Hours	Productivity Score
20	85
15	78
30	92
18	80
25	88
22	86
17	79
28	90
19	82
24	87
21	84
16	77
27	89
23	85
26	88
32	94
14	76
29	91
20	83
31	93
33	95
35	97
18	79
19	81
34	96
20	84
25	87
30	92
22	85
26	89

The connection of widgets for the workflow is shown in Fig. 5.7:

Result 1 and Result 2 are given in Figs. 5.8, 5.9, and 5.10, respectively.

Result 2 outcome is given as:

The graph is given as under:

Thus, the equation for the *Productivity Score* is:

$$Productivity\ Score = 63.22 + 0.971 \times (Training\ Hours)$$

The outcome states that for every 1 h of training, the productivity score increases by 0.971 units.

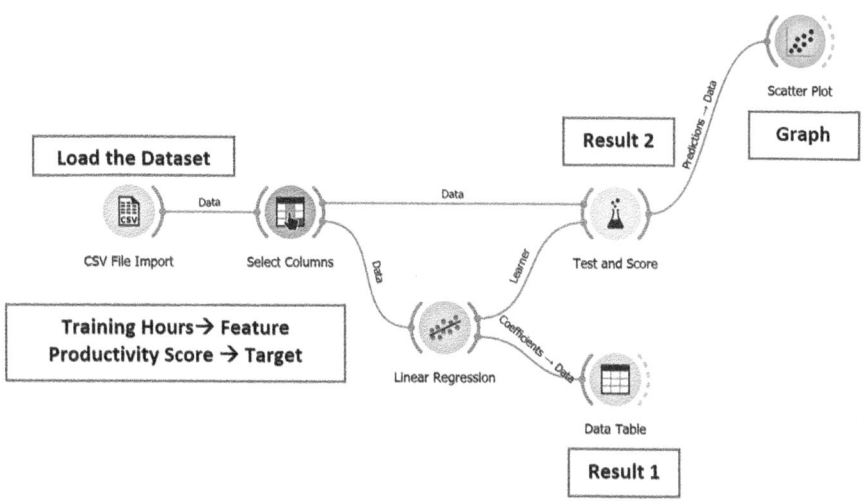

Fig. 5.7 Simple linear regression (Example 5.1)

Fig. 5.8 Value of intercept
and coefficients

	name	coef
1	intercept	63.122
2	Training Hours	0.971266

Model	MSE	RMSE	MAE	MAPE	R2
Linear Regression	0.684	0.827	0.625	0.007	0.979

Fig. 5.9 The value of R^2 for Example 5.1

Multiple Linear Regression

Multiple linear regression is used to predict one outcome (or dependent variable) based on the multiple independent variables. In simple terms, multiple linear regression helps to understand how several factors might affect something we want to predict.

The mathematical equation for multiple linear regression is given by Eq. (5.2)

$$Y = b_0 + b_1 * X_1 + b_2 * X_2 + \ldots + b_n * X_n \tag{5.2}$$

where

Y: represents the predicted outcome (dependent variable).
$X_1, X_2, \ldots, X_n$: are the set of independent variables.

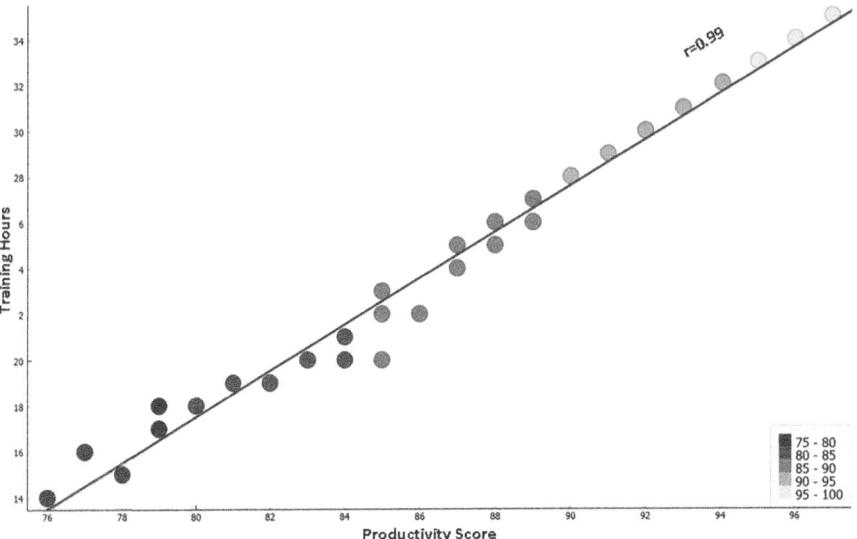

Fig. 5.10 The R^2 graph for Example 5.1

b_0: is the intercept, which is the value of Y when all the independent variables are zero.

b_1, b_2, …, b_n: are the coefficients, indicating how much each independent variable influences the outcome.

In simple words, the equation tells us that the predicted outcome, Y, is a combination of the intercept with the influence of each independent variable (X_1, X_2, etc.) weighted by their respective coefficients (b_1, b_2, etc.).

The goal in multiple linear regression is to find the best values for the coefficients (b_0, b_1, b_2, etc.) that minimize the difference between the predicted outcomes and the actual data.

Example 5.2:

A company wants to understand how Years of Experience (Y), Training Hours (T), and Meeting Attended (M) by the employee impact the employee productivity (E). The company collected 50 data points to build a predictive model using multiple linear regression.

The equation of multiple linear regression is

$$E = b_0 + b_1.Y + b_2.T + b_3.M$$

The sample dataset is:

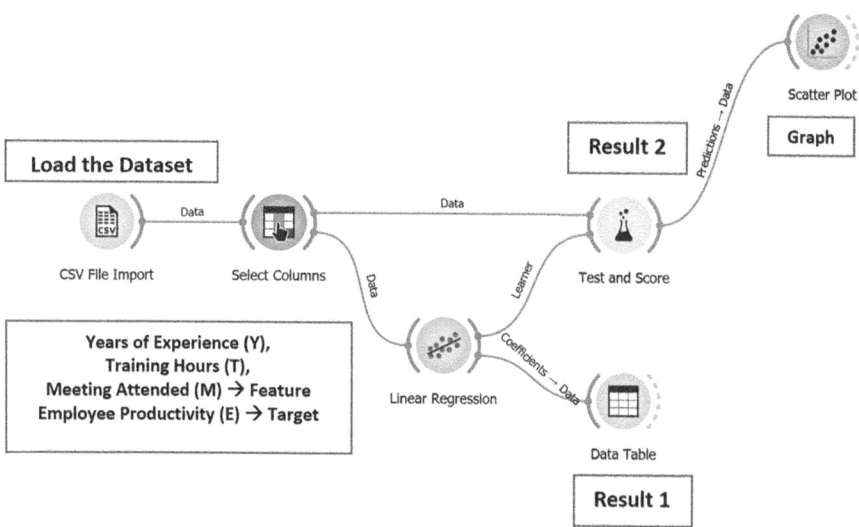

Fig. 5.11 The workflow for multiple linear regression (Example 5.2)

Fig. 5.12 Value of
intercept and coefficients

	name	coef
1	intercept	58.9847
2	Training Hours	0.584013
3	Years of Experie...	4.7876
4	Meetings Atten...	-0.0180622

Employee ID	Years of experience	Training hours	Meetings attended	Employee productivity
1	3	20	4	85
2	5	15	3	92
3	7	30	5	110
4	2	10	2	78
5	8	25	4	115
6	4	18	3	90
7	6	22	4	100
8	3	12	2	80
9	9	35	6	120
10	5	21	4	98
11	7	28	5	105
12	4	16	3	88

The workflow is shown in Fig. 5.11:

Result 1 and Result 2 are given in Figs. 5.12, 5.13, and 5.14, respectively.

Result 2 outcome is given as:

Model	MSE	RMSE	MAE	MAPE	R2
Linear Regression	4.772	2.184	1.674	0.017	0.980

Fig. 5.13 The value of R^2 for Example 5.2

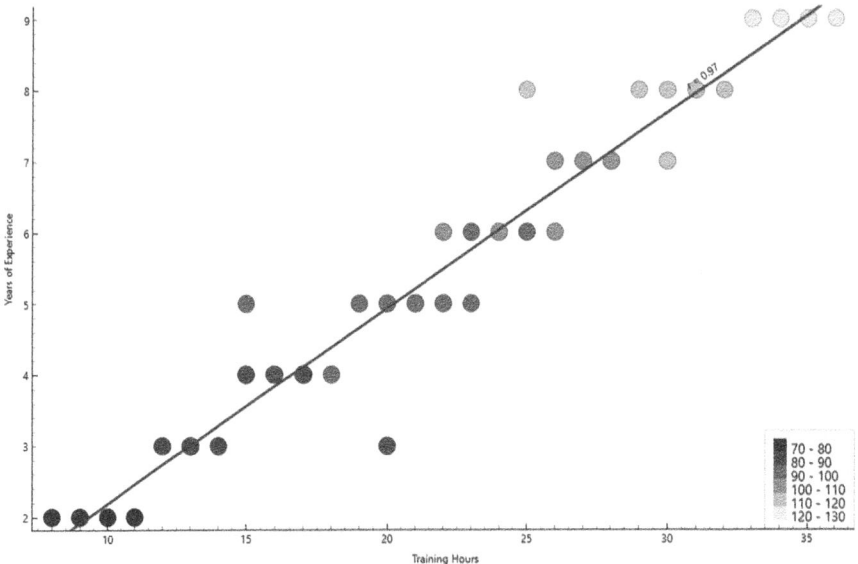

Fig. 5.14 The R^2 graph for Example 5.2

The graph is given as under:
The equation for the Employee *Productivity* is:

$$E = 56.9847 + 0.58 \times (T) + 4.79\,(Y) - 0.01(M)$$

This regression model suggests that E depends on the values of T, Y, and M. Positive coefficients (like 0.58 for T and 4.79 for Y) increase E, while the negative coefficient (-0.01 for M) decreases E. The intercept 56.9847 is the starting value of E when all variables are zero.

Supervised Learning: Binary classification
The binary classification is the type of supervised learning, where the aim is to divide the data into one of two groups or class. The three main types of binary classification are given in Fig. 5.15.

The outcomes of the binary classification are evaluated using confusion matrix, as shown in Fig. 5.16.

From Fig. 5.16, it is clear that correct prediction is given by Eqs. 5.3a and 5.3b

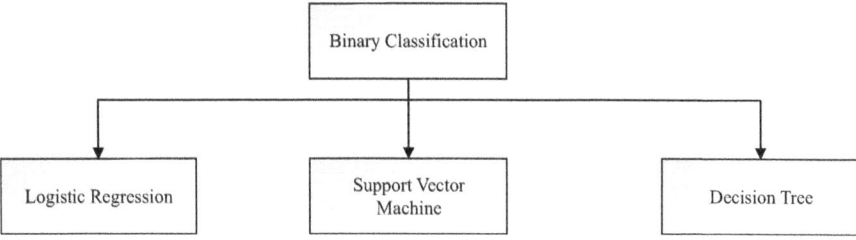

Fig. 5.15 Binary classification

Fig. 5.16 Evaluation of confusion matrix for classification algorithms (Source: Evidently AI, 2024)

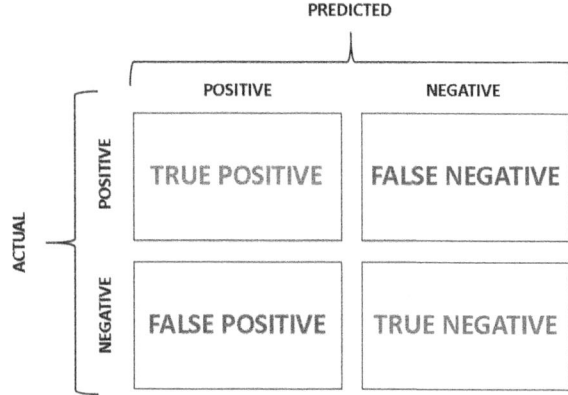

Correct Prediction

$$= \frac{(\text{True Positive} + \text{True Negative})}{(\text{True Positive} + \text{False positive} + \text{False Negative} + \text{False Positive})} \quad (5.3a)$$

Incorrect Prediction

$$= \frac{(\text{False negative} + \text{False positive})}{(\text{True Positive} + \text{False positive} + \text{False Negative} + \text{False Positive})} \quad (5.3b)$$

Logistic Regression

Logistic regression is a classification procedure that is frequently used when the dependent variable is binary (i.e., 0 or 1, True or False, Yes or No). Instead of responding with Yes or No, logistic regression calculates the likelihood and then converts it into one of the two categories. If the probability exceeds a particular threshold (usually 0.5), the answer is yes or no. Figure 5.17 depicts the approach of logistic regression:

There are five steps computing logistic regression in Orange data mining tool as given below:

Step 1: Select Data
Step 2: Feature Selection (select independent and dependent variables)

Fig. 5.17 Approach of logistic regression (Source: Ansari, 2023)

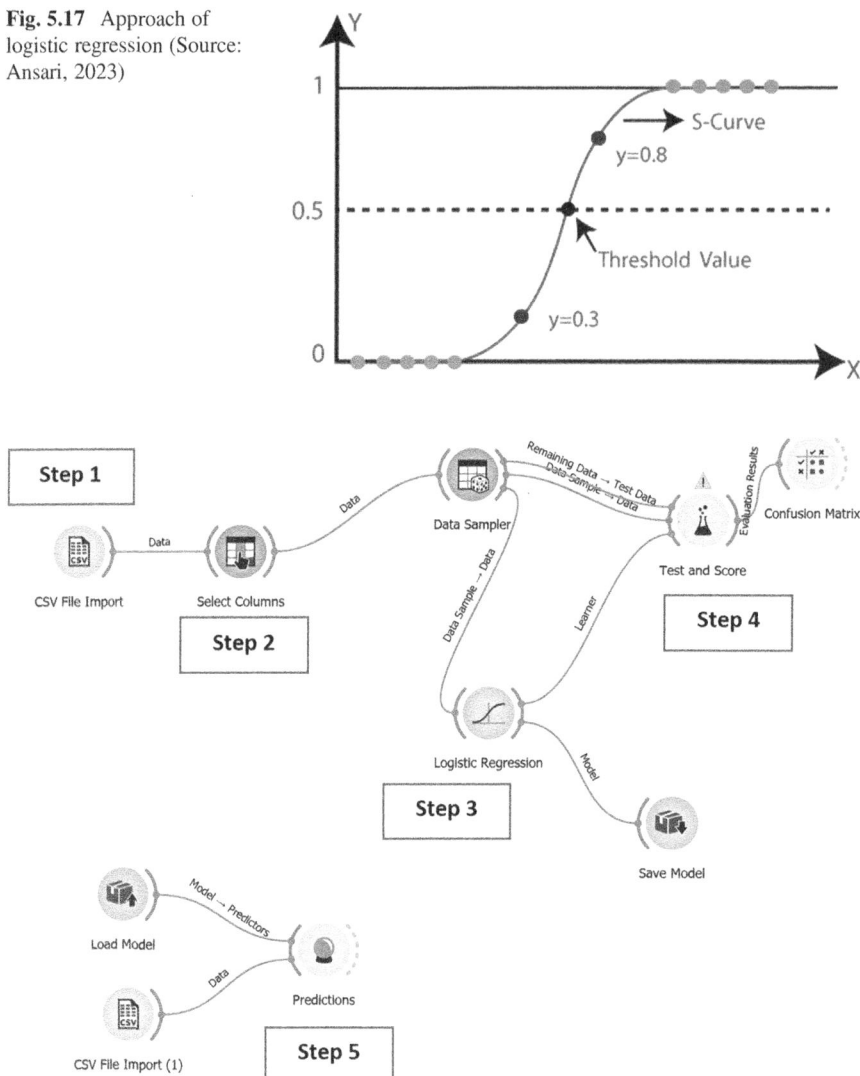

Fig. 5.18 Steps of logistic regression in Orange

Step 3: Split Data and Model Training
Step 4: Model Evaluation
Step 5: Interpret Results

The complete steps in Orange are given in Fig. 5.18.

Example 5.3:

The marketing team of the company wants to predict whether the number of emails sent to consumer and the time spent in minutes by consumer lead them to purchase or not. The company collected the data and the format of the data is given as under:

Customer	Number of emails Sent	Time spent on Website (minutes)	Purchase (Outcome)
1	3	15	0
2	2	10	0
..	..	..	..
..	..	..	..
30	5	29	1

The outcomes of the model show that for 70% train data and 30% test data, the confusion matrix is given by Fig. 5.19a, b

From both the train and test data, the accuracy prediction is 100%. The outcome is shown in Fig. 5.20:

The data demonstrates that if a consumer reads an email less than twice and spends less time on the website, he is unlikely to purchase, but, if a customer spends more time on the website and receives more emails, he is more likely to buy.

Support Vector Machine (SVM)

For classification problems, a supervised machine learning approach called Support Vector Machines (SVM) can also be used. The model's primary objective is to identify the optimal decision boundary, also known as a hyperplane, which divides the data into distinct classes. As shown in Fig. 5.21, SVM determines the line or hyperplane that best divides two classes:

As shown in Fig. 5.22, SVM creates many hyperplanes to divide the data if there are more than two classes while optimizing its border between each class:

The steps of computing SVM in Orange data mining tool are given below:

Step 1: Select Data

Step 2: Feature Selection (select independent and dependent variables)

We need to select two features, x_1 and x_2, and the goal is to use these features to predict the class labels.

Step 3: Use SVM for prediction

In this step, we use SVM to find the optimal hyperplane that separates the two features. The equation of the hyperplane is given by Eq. (5.4)

$$w_1x_1 + w_2x_2 + b = 0 \tag{5.4}$$

and $w = [w_1, w_2]$ are the weights, and b is the bias term.

Step 4: Model Evaluation

Step 5: Interpret Results

The complete steps in Orange are given in Fig. 5.23.

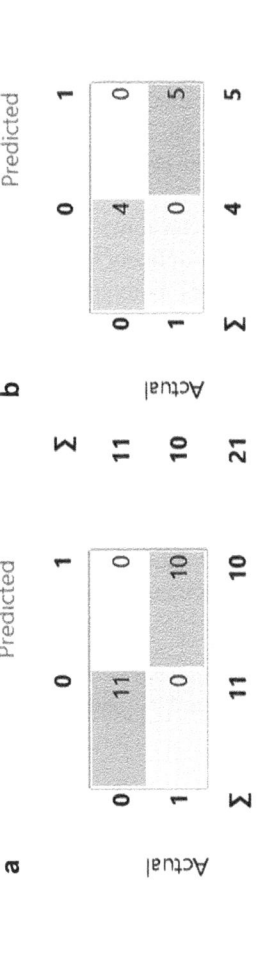

Fig. 5.19 (a) Confusion matrix—logistic regression for train data. (b) Confusion matrix—logistic regression for test data

⬛ Predictions - Orange

Show probabilities for [Classes known to the model   ⌄]

Logistic Regression	Number of Emails Se	Sent on Website (r	Unnamed: 3
1 0.06 : 0.94 → 1	3	18	?
2 0.00 : 1.00 → 1	4	27	?
3 0.95 : 0.05 → 0	2	13	?
4 1.00 : 0.00 → 0	1	8	?
5 0.00 : 1.00 → 1	5	31	?

Fig. 5.20 Predictions of logistic algorithm

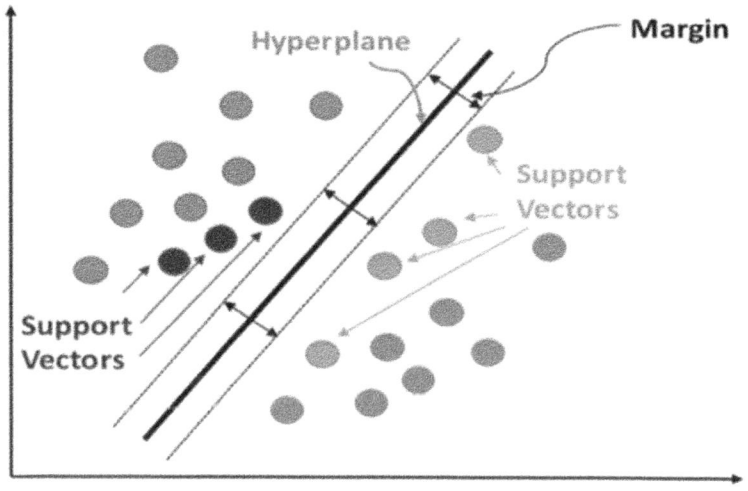

Fig. 5.21 SVM with two classes (Source: Datatron, 2021)

Example 5.4:
Imagine that the marketing team is interested in predicting whether a customer will make a purchase based on certain features (age, gender, and estimated salary). The prediction is crucial for targeted marketing strategies, allowing the company to focus its efforts on potential customers who are more likely to make a purchase. The goal is to build a predictive model to classify customers into two classes: those who make a purchase (Purchased = 1) and those who do not make a purchase (Purchased = 0).

Fig. 5.22 SVM with
multiple classes (Source:
Baeldung, 2020)

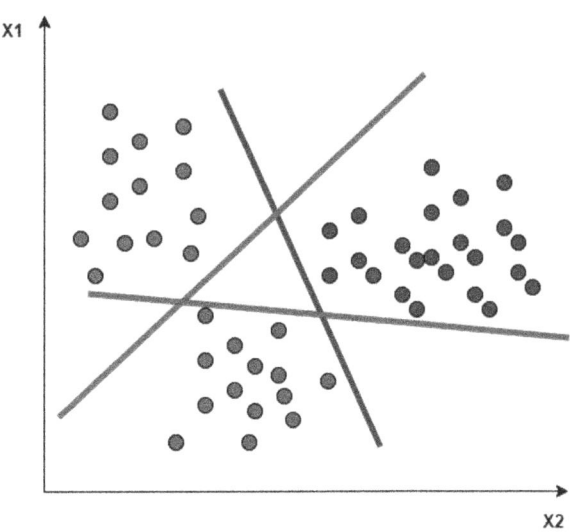

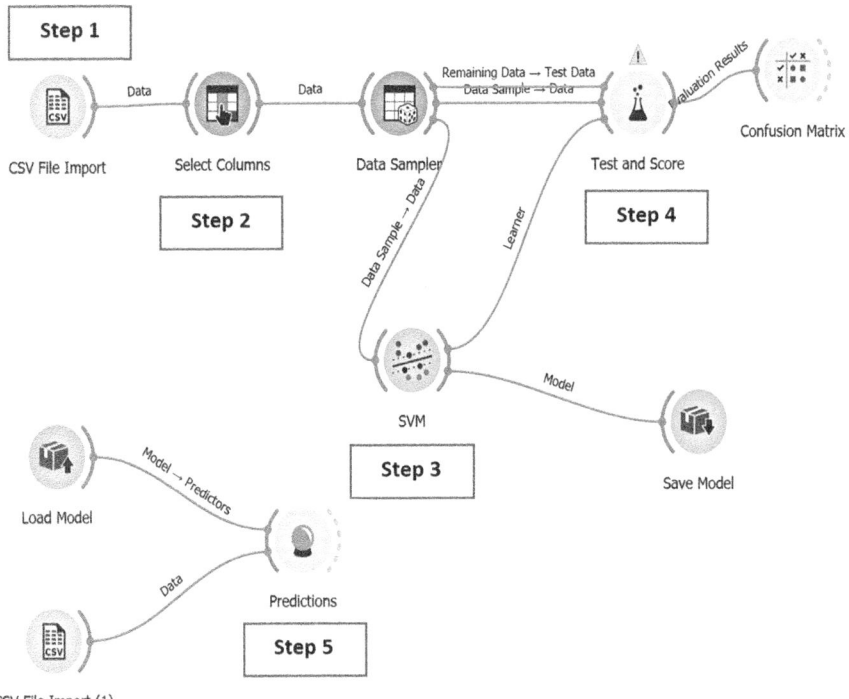

Fig. 5.23 Steps of SVM in Orange

Fig. 5.24 (a) AUC for the 70% train data. (b) AUC for the 30% test data

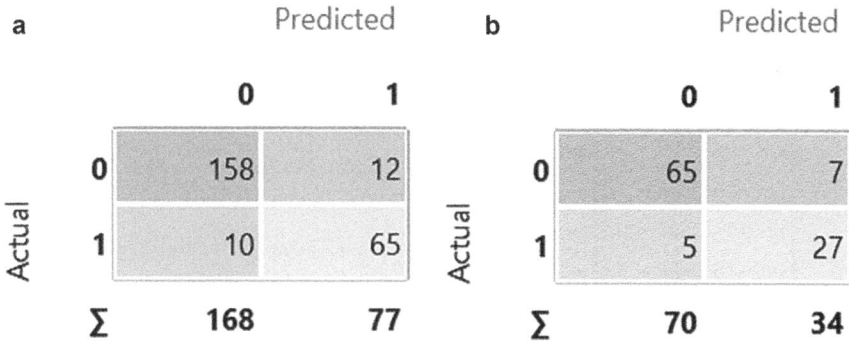

Fig. 5.25 (a) Confusion matrix—SVM for train data. (b) Confusion matrix—SVM for test data

The tabular representation of the data:

User ID	Gender	Age	Estimated salary	Purchased
15624510	Male	19	19,000	0
15810944	Male	35	20,000	0
15668575	Female	26	43,000	0
..	...	..	..	..
15579212	Male	39	77,000	0

The Test and Score widget from Fig. 5.23 gives the accuracy of the SVM model that adopted the business scenario. For the training data, the value of AUC is 0.953, indicating that the predictive model gives 95.3% correct predictions for the 70% train dataset. For the remaining 30% dataset, the value of AUC is 0.967, indicating 96.7% of correct predictions (Fig. 5.24).

The outcomes of the model show that for 70% train data and 30% test data, the confusion matrix is given by Fig. 5.25a, b.

From Eqs. 5.3a and 5.3b, for the 70% train data, there are 91.02% correct predictions and 8.98% incorrect predictions. For the 30% test data, 88.46% are correct predictions and 11.54% are incorrect predictions.

Predictions - Orange

Show probabilities for   Classes known to the model ⌄

	SVM	Gender	Age	EstimatedSalary
1	0.97 : 0.03 → 0	Male	38	61000
2	0.27 : 0.73 → 1	Female	38	113000
3	0.95 : 0.05 → 0	Male	37	75000
4	0.60 : 0.40 → 0	Female	42	90000
5	0.97 : 0.03 → 0	Female	37	57000
6	0.58 : 0.42 → 0	Male	36	99000
7	0.03 : 0.97 → 1	Male	60	34000
8	0.16 : 0.84 → 1	Male	54	70000
9	0.88 : 0.12 → 0	Female	41	72000
10	0.93 : 0.07 → 0	Male	40	71000
11	0.89 : 0.11 → 0	Male	42	54000
12	0.04 : 0.96 → 1	Male	43	129000
13	0.13 : 0.87 → 1	Female	53	34000
14	0.57 : 0.43 → 0	Female	47	50000
15	0.78 : 0.22 → 0	Female	42	79000
16	0.26 : 0.74 → 1	Male	42	104000
17	0.06 : 0.94 → 1	Female	59	29000
18	0.09 : 0.91 → 1	Female	58	47000
19	0.46 : 0.54 → 1	Male	46	88000

Fig. 5.26 Predictions of SVM algorithm

From both the train and test data, the accuracy prediction is above 85% (91.02% and 88.46%). The outcome is shown in Fig. 5.26:

The result of 0.97 for the first row in Fig. 5.26 indicates a 97% likelihood of class 0 and a 3% possibility of class 1. This indicates that the customer will not make a purchase. The marketing team may also determine which customers will buy from each row accordingly.

Decision Tree

Decision tree is a basic and readily comprehended machine learning technique that is used for both classification and regression tasks. It works by recursively partitioning the dataset into subgroups depending on the most significant properties or features.

There are five steps of computing decision tree as given below:

Step 1: Select Data
Step 2: Feature Selection (select independent and dependent variables)

We need to select two features, x_1 and x_2, and the goal is to use these features to predict the class labels.

Step 3: Start at the Root (Node 0):

At the beginning, we have all the data, which we can represent as Node 0.

Choose the Best Split (Node 1):

To decide how to split the data, we select an attribute (X) and a threshold value (T). This split can be represented as a condition:

$$X < T \; or \; X > \, = T.$$

Split the Data (Nodes 1a and 1b):

All the data that meets the condition $X < T$ goes into one branch (Node 1a), and all the data that meets $X > \, = T$ goes into the other branch (Node 1b).

Repeat for Each Branch:

For each branch, we repeat steps 2 and 3, selecting a new attribute and threshold to split the data further. Each split is a new node, like Node 2, Node 3, and so on.

Keep Going Until we reach Terminal Nodes:

We continue this process, splitting data at each node until we reach terminal nodes (also known as leaves). These nodes don't split the data further and represent the final outcome or prediction.

Step 4: Model Evaluation

Step 5: Interpret Results

The complete steps in Orange are given in Fig. 5.27.

Example 5.5:

Assume, a company is deciding whether to hire a job applicant based on their qualifications. The company has collected data on past hires to understand what factors contribute to a successful hire.

Attributes (Features):

- Years of experience: The number of years of experience the applicant has.
- Education level: The highest level of education (Bachelor's, Master's, or Ph.D.).
- Technical skills: A measure of the applicant's technical skills (e.g., on a scale of 1–10).
- Target (Outcome):
    Hire Decision: Whether the applicant should be hired [Yes (1) or No (0)].

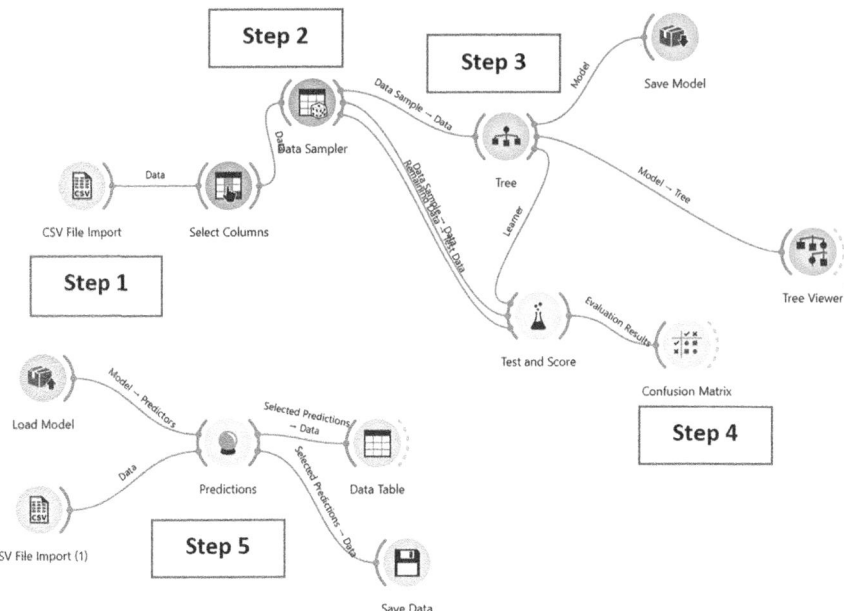

Fig. 5.27 Steps of Decision Tree in Orange

The format of dataset for the hiring decision is as follows:

Applicant	Years of experience	Education level	Technical skills	Hire decision
1	1	1	5	0
2	2	2	8	1
3	0.5	3	6	1
4	3	1	4	0
...	...	...	...	...
...	...	...	...	...
...	...	...	...	...
...	...	...	...	...
...	...	...	...	...
100	1.4	2	2	0

In this dataset, we have 100 job applicants, each with their years of experience, education level [(1=Bachelors, 2=Master's, and 3=Ph.D.)], technical skills (1–10), and a hire decision [Yes (1) or No (0)].

After following the steps as mentioned in Fig. 5.27, we get the following decision tree for 70% of the train dataset and 30% of the test dataset in Fig. 5.28a, b.

The outcomes of the confusion matrix for the train and test data are given in Fig. 5.29a, b.

The prediction of the decision tree is shown in Fig. 5.30:

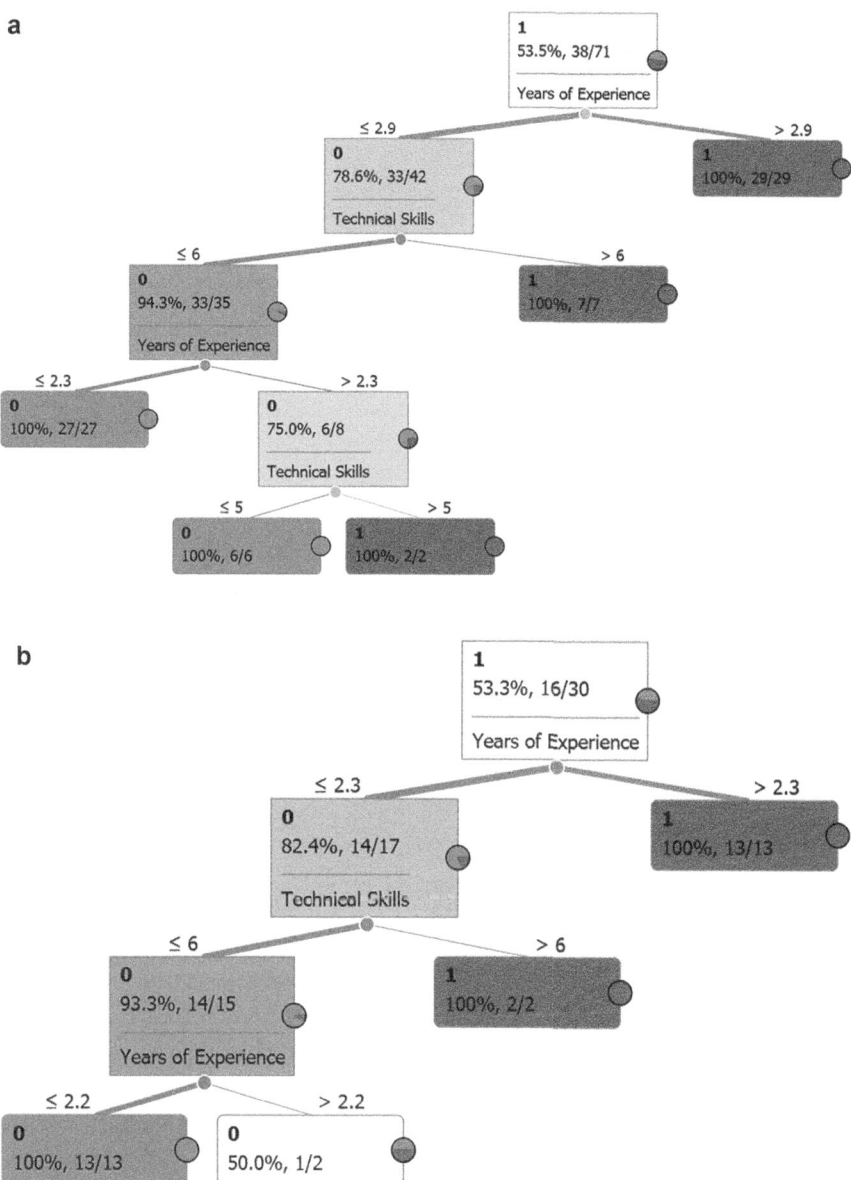

Fig. 5.28 (**a**) Outcomes of decision tree (70% train dataset). (**b**) Outcomes of decision tree (30% test dataset)

From Fig. 5.27, if we click Data Table widget, we get the following outcome as shown in Fig. 5.31.

a   Predicted   **b**   Predicted

		0	1	Σ
	0	100.0 %	0.0 %	33
Actual	1	0.0 %	100.0 %	38
	Σ	33	38	71

		0	1	Σ
	0	93.3 %	0.0 %	14
Actual	1	6.7 %	100.0 %	16
	Σ	15	15	30

Fig. 5.29 (**a**) Confusion matrix—decision tree for train data. (**b**) Confusion matrix—decision tree for test data

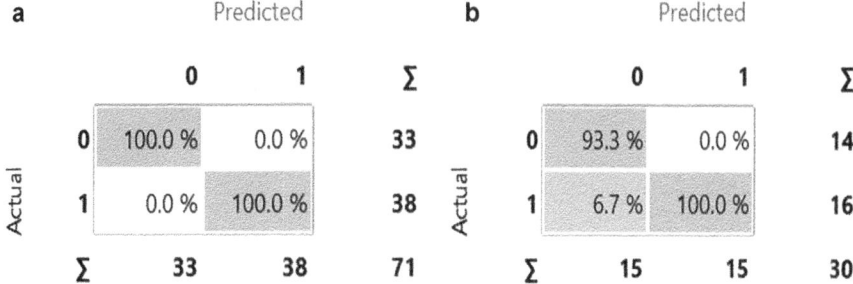

Predictions - Orange

Show probabilities for (None)

	Tree	Applicant	Years of Experienc	Education Level	Technical Skills
1	0	1	2.8	1	5
2	1	2	3.7	3	7
3	0	3	0.6	2	6
4	1	4	4.6	1	8
5	0	5	2.7	3	4
6	1	6	3.4	2	7
7	0	7	1.9	1	3
8	1	8	2.5	3	6
9	0	9	0.5	2	6
10	1	10	4.7	1	9
11	0	11	2.6	3	5
12	1	12	3.3	2	7
13	0	13	1.7	1	2
14	0	14	2.3	3	6
15	0	15	0.4	2	6
16	1	16	4.8	1	8
17	0	17	2.9	3	4
1.	1	1.	..	.	7

Fig. 5.30 Predictions of decision tree

The outcomes clearly indicate that applicants with *years of experience ≥ 2.9 years and Education Level = 1(Bachelors) and Technical skills ≥ 7* are most likely to be hired by the company.

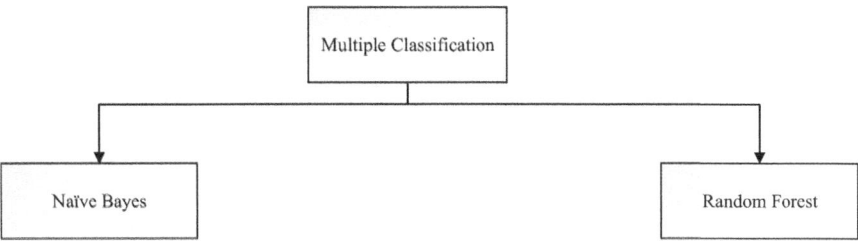

	Tree	Applicant	'ears of Experienc(	Education Level	Technical Skills
1	1	25	2.9	1	7

Fig. 5.31 Outcomes of the decision tree

Fig. 5.32 Multiple classification

Supervised Learning: Multiple classification

Multiple classification is a type of supervised learning in which the objective is to classify data into one of many groups or categories. Figure 5.32 depicts the two types of multiple classification.

The outcomes of multiple classification are also evaluated using a confusion matrix.

Naïve Bayes

Naive Bayes is an algorithm that uses Bayes' theorem to do multiple classification tasks. It considers that each feature is independent, allowing it to rapidly and effectively categorize data into multiple categories.

There are five steps computing Naïve Bayes in Orange data mining tool as given below:

Step 1: Select Data
Step 2: Feature Selection (convert all columns into categorical variables, and the select independent and dependent variables)
Step 3: Split Data and Model Training
Step 4: Model Evaluation
Step 5: Interpret Results

The complete steps in Orange are given in Fig. 5.33.

Example 5.6:

Assume the company wants to predict customer's *purchase preference* for different types of products (Electronics, Clothing, and Groceries) based on *Age Group*, *Income Level*, and *Previous Purchases*. The format of dataset is given as:

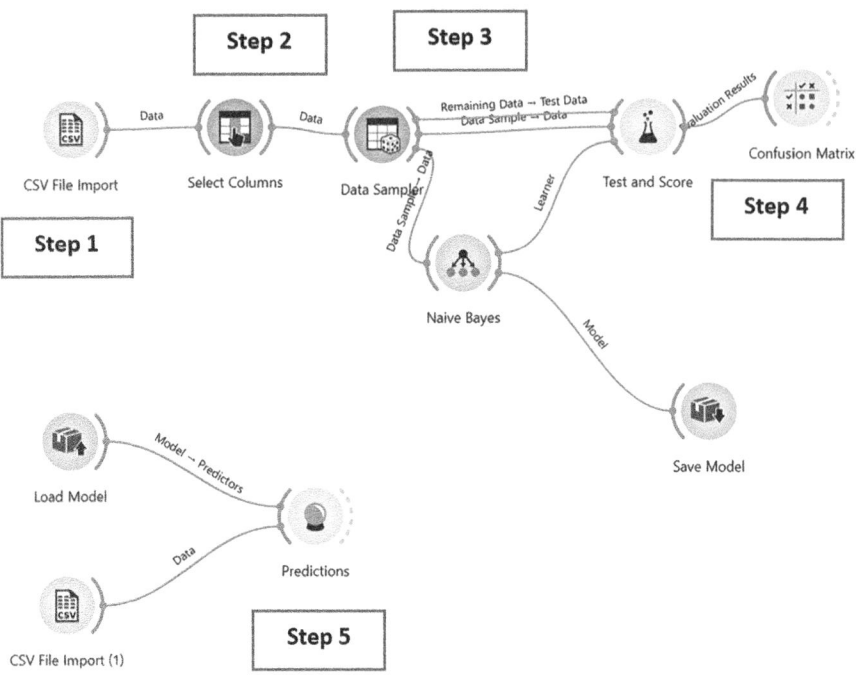

Fig. 5.33 Steps of Naïve Bayes tree in Orange

Age Group	Income Level	Previous Purchases	Purchase Preference
Young	Low	2	Groceries
Middle	High	5	Electronics
Senior	Medium	4	Clothing
Young	Medium	3	Groceries
Middle	Low	1	Groceries
Senior	High	6	Electronics
Young	Low	2	Groceries
Middle	Medium	3	Clothing
Senior	Low	1	Groceries
Young	High	4	Electronics
Middle	Medium	4	Electronics
Senior	Medium	5	Clothing
Young	Medium	2	Groceries
Middle	High	6	Electronics
Senior	Low	2	Groceries
Young	Low	3	Groceries
Middle	Medium	3	Clothing
Senior	High	5	Electronics
Young	High	4	Electronics
Middle	Low	2	Groceries

Fig. 5.34 (**a**) Confusion matrix—Naïve Bayes for train data. (**b**) Confusion matrix—Naïve Bayes for test data

🏦 Predictions - Orange

Show probabilities for [Classes known to the model   ⌄]

	Naive Bayes	Age Group	Income Level	Previous Purchase
1	0.58 : 0.04 : 0.38 → Clothing	Young	Medium	3
2	0.10 : 0.06 : 0.84 → Groceries	Middle	Low	2
3	0.16 : 0.81 : 0.03 → Electronics	Senior	High	5
4	0.07 : 0.03 : 0.90 → Groceries	Young	Low	1
5	0.10 : 0.87 : 0.03 → Electronics	Middle	High	6
6	0.52 : 0.35 : 0.13 → Clothing	Senior	Medium	4
7	0.20 : 0.67 : 0.13 → Electronics	Young	High	5
8	0.79 : 0.08 : 0.13 → Clothing	Middle	Medium	3
9	0.10 : 0.07 : 0.83 → Groceries	Senior	Low	2
10	0.41 : 0.18 : 0.40 → Clothing	Young	Medium	4

Fig. 5.35 Predictions based on Naïve Bayes model

In the dataset, Purchase Preference is the target variable with three options (Electronics, Clothing, and Groceries).

The outcomes of the confusion matrix for the train and test data are given in Fig. 5.34a, b.

From Fig. 5.34a, b, it can be seen that the model executes effectively in the clothing category, with 100% of clothing factors correctly identified. For electronics, 80% of the products are properly classified, whereas 20% are misclassified as clothing. Similarly, 83.3% of groceries are correctly classified, with 16.7% misclassified as clothing. As all the predictions are above 80%, the model can be adopted.

The prediction of the decision tree is shown in Fig. 5.35:

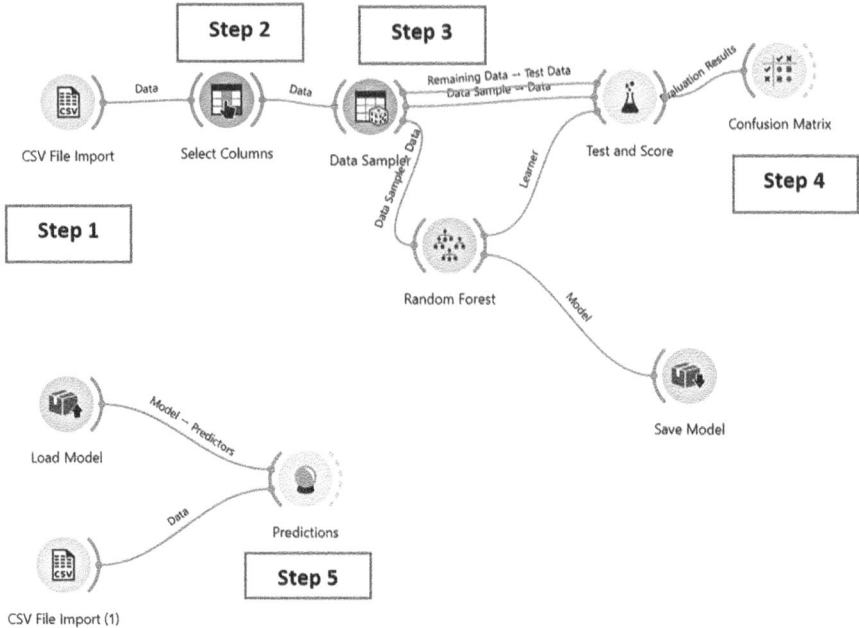

Fig. 5.36 Steps of Random Forest in Orange

The model gives probabilities to each class and selects the one with the highest likelihood as the predicted category. For example, the first record with a young, medium-income individual and three prior transactions has a 58% likelihood of buying clothing. Electronics are expected to be purchased by high-income or senior individuals (e.g., rows 3 and 5), while groceries are often expected for low-income groups. This suggests that the model recognizes a link between customer demographics, previous purchasing history, and preferred product categories.

Random Forest
Random Forest is a decision-tree-based approach to making predictions. Random Forest performs effectively for multiple classification problems since it averages the results of independent trees to minimize errors.

There are five steps computing Random Forest in Orange data mining tool as given below:

Step 1: Select Data
Step 2: Feature Selection (select independent and dependent variables)
Step 3: Split Data and Model Training
Step 4: Model Evaluation
Step 5: Interpret Results

The complete steps in Orange are given in Fig. 5.36

Example 5.7:
This dataset represents customer information for a telecom company, capturing attributes like age, monthly charges, contract length, data usage, and support calls, to predict customer churn risk categories (e.g., "No," "Likely Churn," "High Churn Risk," "Long-term") and help the company improve retention strategies. The format of dataset is given as:

Customer ID	Age	Monthly charges ($)	Contract length (months)	Data usage (GB)	Support Calls	Churn (Target)
1	35	60	12	2.5	2	No
2	42	75	24	3.2	1	Likely Churn
3	28	50	6	1.8	3	No
4	55	85	36	4.5	0	Long-term
5	32	70	12	2	2	No
6	45	90	24	3.8	1	Likely Churn
7	29	55	6	1.5	3	No
8	58	100	36	4.8	0	Long-term
9	38	65	12	2.2	2	No
10	50	80	24	3.5	1	High Churn Risk
11	27	45	6	1.2	3	No
12	60	110	36	5	0	Long-term
13	36	55	12	2.3	2	No
14	48	85	24	3.7	1	Likely Churn
15	31	60	6	1.7	3	No
16	54	95	36	4.2	0	Long-term
17	40	70	12	2.6	2	No
18	52	100	24	3.9	1	High Churn Risk
19	33	50	6	1.4	3	No
20	56	90	36	4.6	0	Long-term
21	37	65	12	2.1	2	No
22	49	80	24	3.6	1	High Churn Risk
23	30	55	6	1.3	3	No
24	57	110	36	4.9	0	Long-term
25	34	60	12	2.4	2	No

a

Actual	High Churn Risk	Likely Churn	Long-term	No
High Churn Risk	100.0 %	0.0 %	0.0 %	0.0 %
Likely Churn	0.0 %	100.0 %	0.0 %	0.0 %
Long-term	0.0 %	0.0 %	100.0 %	0.0 %
No	0.0 %	0.0 %	0.0 %	100.0 %
∑	2	2	4	10

b

Predicted

Actual	High Churn Risk	Likely Churn	Long-term	No
High Churn Risk	100.0 %	0.0 %	0.0 %	0.0 %
Likely Churn	0.0 %	0.0 %	0.0 %	100.0 %
Long-term	0.0 %	0.0 %	100.0 %	0.0 %
No	0.0 %	0.0 %	0.0 %	100.0 %
∑	1	0	2	4

Fig. 5.37 (**a**) Confusion matrix—random forest for train data. (**b**) Confusion matrix—random forest for test data

 Predictions - Orange

Show probabilities for Classes known to the model   ⌄

	Random Forest	Age	Monthly Charges (!	tract Length (Mor	Data Usage (GB)	Support Calls
1	0.00 : 0.00 : 0.00 : 1.00 → No	39	70	12	2.7	2
2	0.30 : 0.39 : 0.17 : 0.13 → Likely Churn	43	85	24	3.3	1
3	0.00 : 0.00 : 0.00 : 1.00 → No	29	55	6	1.6	3
4	0.18 : 0.12 : 0.70 : 0.00 → Long-term	61	100	36	5.1	0
5	0.00 : 0.00 : 0.00 : 1.00 → No	37	65	12	2.4	2
6	0.39 : 0.44 : 0.17 : 0.00 → Likely Churn	46	90	24	3.9	1
7	0.00 : 0.00 : 0.00 : 1.00 → No	33	60	6	1.9	3
8	0.18 : 0.12 : 0.70 : 0.00 → Long-term	55	95	36	4.3	0
9	0.30 : 0.39 : 0.17 : 0.13 → Likely Churn	42	80	24	3.4	1
10	0.00 : 0.00 : 0.00 : 1.00 → No	28	50	6	1.5	3

Fig. 5.38 Predictions based on random forest model

In the dataset, Churn is the target variable with three options (No, Likely Churn, High Churn Risk, Long-term). The meaning of each of the classification categories is:

- *No*: Customer is not likely to churn.
- *Likely Churn*: Customer shows moderate signs of potential churn.
- *High Churn Risk*: Customer shows significant signs of churn risk.
- *Long-Term*: Customer is unlikely to churn and appears stable with long-term engagement.

The outcomes of the confusion matrix for the train and test data are given in Fig. 5.37a, b.

From Fig. 5.37b, it can be observed that the classification is incorrect for likely churn (the sample size=1), but for rest of the parameters, the observations are 100% correct.

The prediction of the decision tree is shown in Fig. 5.38:

Based on Fig. 5.38, we can observe that greater risk of churn ("Likely Churn") is connected with customers who have higher monthly prices, more frequent support calls, shorter contract terms, and moderate to high data use. On the other side, customers forecasted as "No" churn tend to have longer contract terms and fewer support calls, suggesting higher stability with the service. "Long-term" customers display moderate monthly rates, moderate contract periods, and fewer support calls. These indicators collectively suggest that contract term, support calls, and monthly expenses might be major predictors of customer turnover.

Unsupervised Learning
In unsupervised learning, the algorithm is trained on a dataset without labeled output. In other words, it does not contain clear instruction in the form of "correct answers" throughout training. Instead, the algorithm is looking for patterns within the data on its own.

The fundamental objective of unsupervised learning is to uncover classifications in the data. This is often done using approaches including clustering and dimensionality reduction.

1. *Clustering:* Clustering algorithms combine comparable data points together based on particular qualities or attributes. The two primary techniques for clustering are k-Means Clustering and Hierarchical Clustering.
2. *Dimensionality Reduction:* Unsupervised learning may also minimize the amount of features (dimensions) in a dataset while maintaining as much useful information as feasible. This is important for displaying and analyzing complicated data further analysis. The fundamental model for Dimensionality Reduction is PCA (Principal Component Analysis).

Unsupervised learning is used extensively in different applications, including consumer segmentation, and anomaly detection, among others. It is especially beneficial when we have enormous datasets and we desire to find relationship between data.

k-Means Clustering
K-Means clustering is a prominent unsupervised learning approach used to organize relating data points into groups. The k-means clustering splits a dataset into K clusters, where K is determined by the user, who needs to group data points that are comparable to each other.

Steps for k-means clustering
k-Means clustering can be done in five steps as mentioned below:

Step 1: Identify the number of cluster, which we call k.
Step 2: Calculate the centroid, which represents the center of clusters.

Mathematically, if we have a cluster C_i with n data points, the centroid is computed as given by Eq. (5.5)

$$C_i = \frac{1}{n} \sum_{j=1}^{n} X_j \tag{5.5}$$

where C_i is the centroid of cluster, n is the number of data points in clusters, and $X_j$represents each data point in the cluster.

Step 3: Distance each data objects to clusters

The distance of each data objects (points) to clusters is calculated using Euclidean Distance.

Given a data point as $X_j = (X_1, X_2, \ldots\ldots, X_n)$ and a centroid $C_i = (C_1, C_2, \ldots\ldots, C_n)$, the Euclidean distance is given by Eq. (5.6) as

$$d(X_j, C_i) = \sqrt{\sum_{i=1}^{n} (X_j - C_i)^2} \tag{5.6}$$

Step 4: Grouping based on minimum distance

This step is divided into three parts, which are iterative in nature.

Part 1: We are required to recalculate the centroids for each cluster by taking mean of all data points assigned to the cluster

For cluster C_i

$$C_i = \left(1/|S_i|\right) * \sum X \epsilon S_i X \tag{5.7}$$

where $|S_i|$ is the number of data points in cluster C_i.

Part 2: This part is called Reassignment.

1. Repeat the assignment step using the updated centroids.
2. Continue to iterate between assignment and update until a stopping criterion is met, such as a maximum number of iterations or when the centroids no longer change significantly.

Part 3: This part is called Convergence.

The algorithm converges when the centroids no longer change significantly or when a predefined stopping criterion is met.

Step 5: Output

The final clusters are defined by the data points assigned to each cluster after convergence.

The complete set of five steps is given in Fig. 5.39

The five steps are defined in Orange tool as mentioned in Fig. 5.40:

Example 5.8:

Consider an online retail company that aims to segment its customers to tailor marketing strategies and improve customer engagement. The company has a vast dataset with millions of customer records, but for simplicity, we will focus on a sample of 30 customers. The format of dataset is given as:

Fig. 5.39 Steps of k-Means
algorithm (Source:
TutorialRide, 2022)

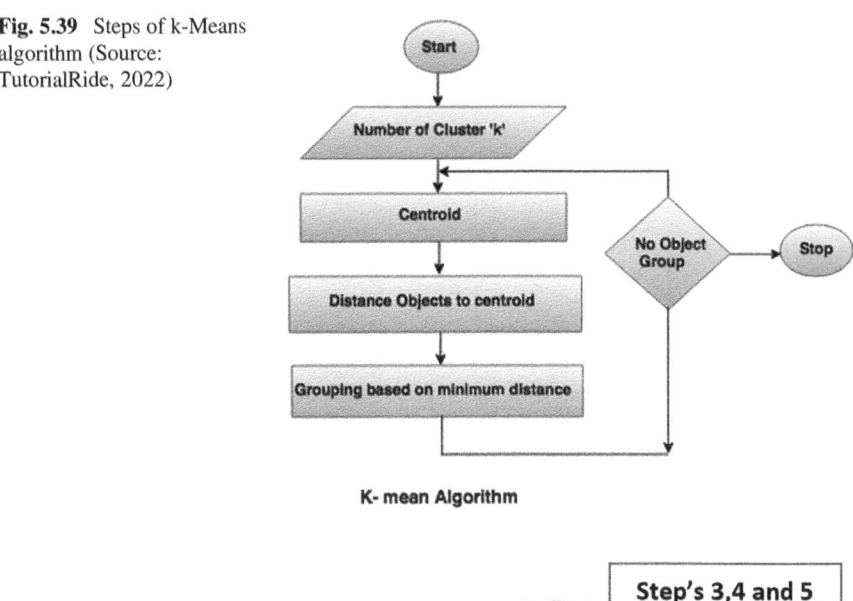

Fig. 5.40 k-Means clustering in Orange

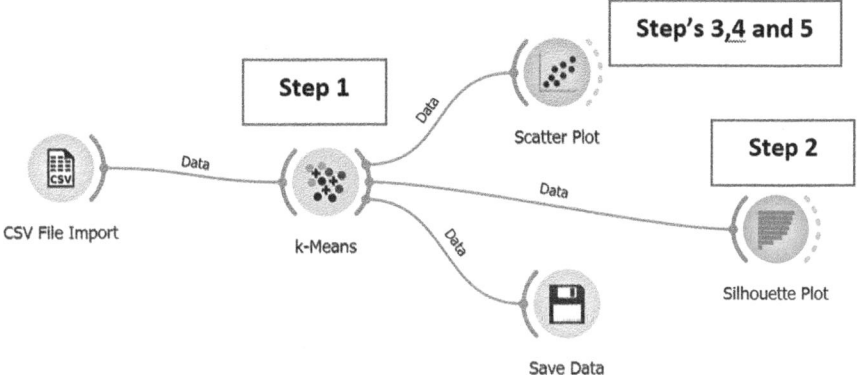

Customer ID	Age	Total Orders	Total Spending ($)	Average Order Value ($)
1	35	12	500	63
2	28	8	320	68
3	45	15	750	56
..	..	..	..	..
..	..	..	..	..
30	27	11	440	83

The retail company intends to segment customers based on their online shopping behavior. The goal is to create targeted marketing strategies and enhance customer engagement.

Fig. 5.41 Silhouette Score

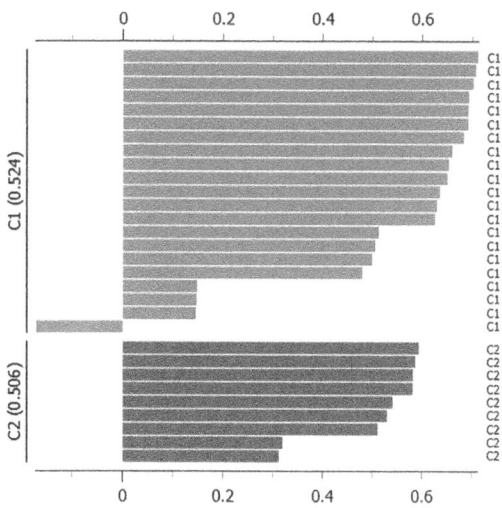

From Fig. 5.40, the outcome of Silhouette Score is mentioned in Fig. 5.41. From the figure above, the Silhouette Score is as follows:

Clusters	Silhouette Score	Analysis
C1	0.524	Between moderate to high
C2	0.506	Moderate

Now, we will scan the results using the scatter plot, Fig. 5.42a–d.
Cluster C1:
Customers are in large number, are of younger age, with less number of orders, spending is on the lower side, and average order value of customer is lower.
Cluster C2:
Customers are less in number, are of older age, with high number of orders, spending is on the higher side, and the average order value of customer is lower.

Hierarchical Clustering
Hierarchical clustering is an approach to arrange and group items that are comparable into clusters. The goal is to establish a hierarchy of clusters, where items that are more identical are grouped together, creating branches of a tree-like structure called a dendrogram.

Steps of Hierarchical Clustering
Hierarchical clustering is an iterative procedure that includes merging or dividing groups depending on their similarity. The two primary approaches are agglomerative (bottom-up) and divisive (top-down). The prevalent technique for hierarchical clustering is the agglomerative approach, with the following six steps:

Step 1: Start with individual data points as clusters

a
Characteristics for Attribute=Age

b
Characteristics for Attribute=Total Orders

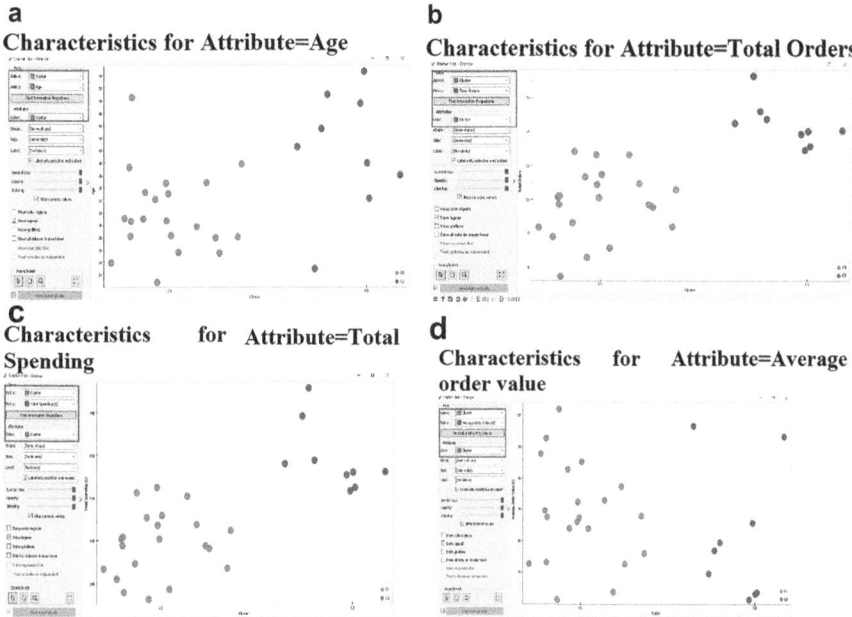

c
Characteristics   for   Attribute=Total Spending

d
Characteristics   for   Attribute=Average order value

Fig. 5.42 (**a**) Clustering using age. (**b**) Clustering using total orders. (**c**) Clustering using total spending. (**d**) Clustering using average order value

Initially, each data point is considered as a separate cluster.

Step 2: Calculate the pairwise distances between clusters

The Euclidean distance for the similarity or dissimilarity between each pair of clusters is mentioned in Eq. (5.8)

$$D\left(C_i, C_j\right) \tag{5.8}$$

C_i and C_j are two clusters and D is the distance between them.

Step 3: Merge the two closest clusters

Combine the two clusters with the smallest distance into a single cluster.

Step 4: Update the distance matrix

Recalculate the distances between the new cluster and all other clusters using an appropriate linkage criterion (e.g., single linkage, complete linkage, average linkage).

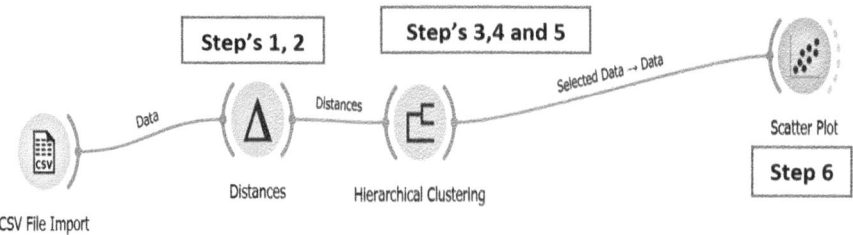

Fig. 5.43 Steps of hierarchical clustering in Orange

$$D(C_{new}, C_k) \tag{5.9}$$

Step 5: Repeat steps 3 and 4 until only a single cluster remains

Continue merging the closest clusters and updating the distance matrix until all data points belong to a single cluster.

Step 6: Output

The outputs are obtained based on the attributes (characteristics).

This process results in a hierarchical tree or dendrogram that shows the relationships between clusters at each step of merging. The height of the dendrogram represents the distance at which clusters were merged.

The six steps are defined in Orange tool as mentioned in Fig. 5.43:

Example 5.9:
The company wants to understand its customer base and tailor marketing strategies to different customer segments. The company collects data customers to divide them based on age, income, and spending behavior.

The format of dataset is as follows:

Customer ID	Age	Annual Income (k$)	Spending Score (1-100)
1	19	15	39
2	21	15	81
3	20	16	6
..	..	..	..
200	30	137	83

After setting the environment and clicking the hierarchical cluster widget, we get five clusters as given in Fig. 5.44.

We will now connect the hierarchical clustering to Scatter Plot, and will observe the outcomes based on the adjustments for the X and Y axis (as given in Fig. 5.45a–c).

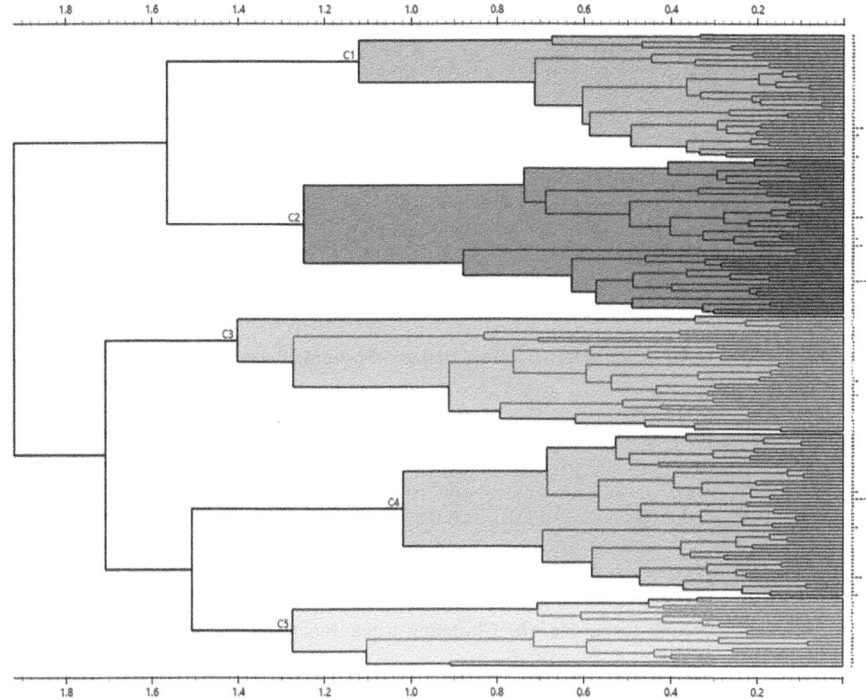

Fig. 5.44 Dendrogram for Example 5.9 (no. of clusters=5)

The recommendations based in Fig. 5.45a–c for the 5 clusters are given below:

Clusters	Recommendations (Tentative)
C1 Middle-aged customers, high income, high spenders	High-end products, loyalty programs
C2 Young customers, low to middle income, varied spenders (high to middle)	Diverse range of products, promotions and discounts
C3 Varied ages, high income, low spenders	Strategies for customer engagement, Promotions and discounts
C4 Varied ages, middle income, middle spenders	Identify needs of customers
C5 Varied ages, low income, low spenders	Cost-effective products

Principal Component Analysis (PCA)

PCA is a dimensionality reduction technique often used to analyze and visualize complex datasets, with the aim of simplifying complex datasets while retaining the important information.

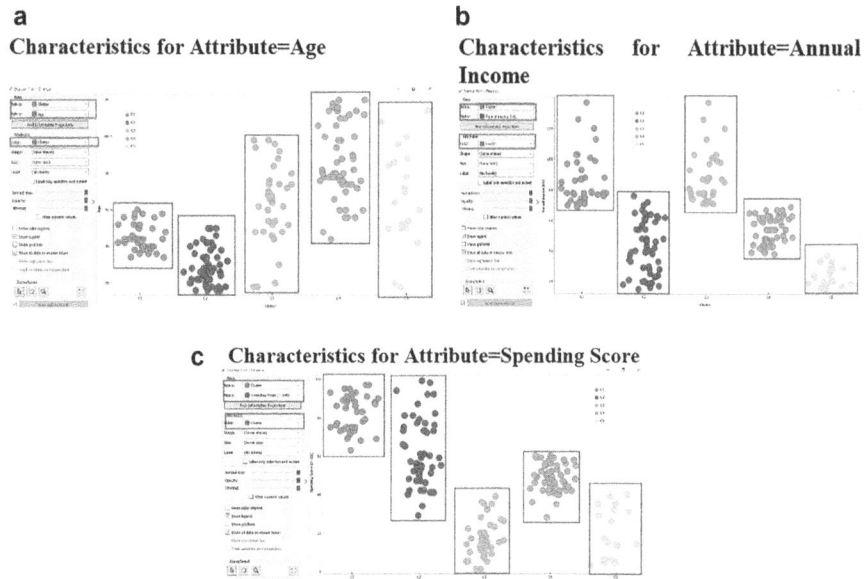

Fig. 5.45 (**a**) Clustering using age. (**b**) Clustering using annual income. (**c**) Clustering using spending score

Dimensionality reduction technique creates a new set of smaller, uncorrelated variables (attributes) from a large dataset. The primary goal is to simplify the data while retaining the essential information required for data analysis.

Steps of PCA

There are five complicated steps of converting the dataset with a large number of attributes to the dataset with a small number of components through PCA. These five steps are shown in Fig. 5.46:

The five steps of PCA in Orange tool are given in Fig. 5.47:

From Fig. 5.47, when we click on *Save Data* widget, we can use four different types of combinations (for two PCs) with the following set of strategies.

Value of PC1	Value of PC2	Strategy
–	–	The company needs to work in all the listed attributes. More emphasis to be given to higher values of PCs
+	–	Focus on successful strategies, while improve upon the negative values of PC2
–	+	Focus on successful strategies, while improve upon the negative values of PC1
+	+	Continue its current strategy, no changes

The table is only valid for two PCs, and the values and strategy change with added number of PCs

We are now ready for data analysis.

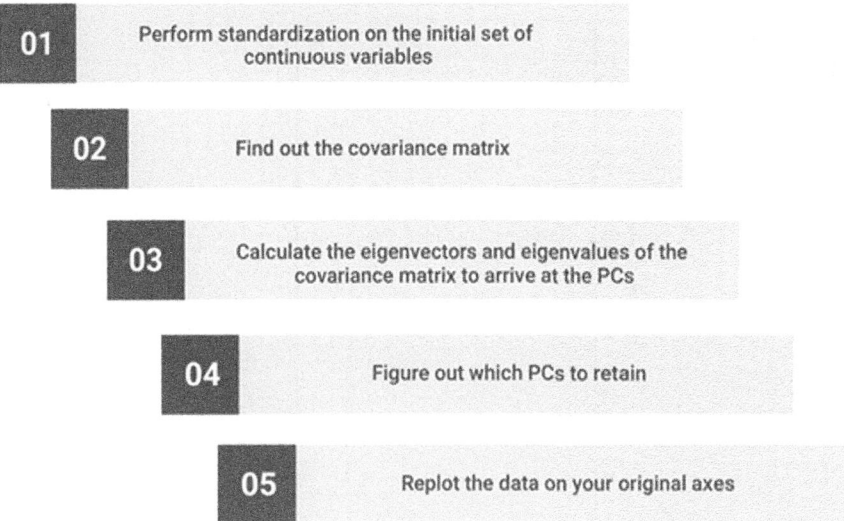

Fig. 5.46 Steps of PCA (Source: Mallick, 2023)

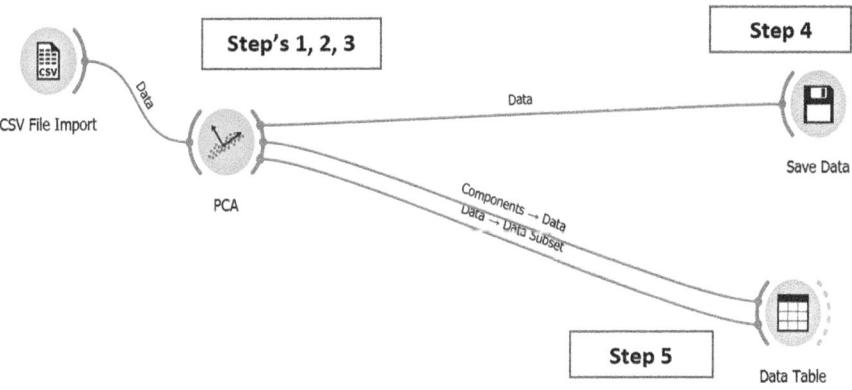

Fig. 5.47 PCA in Orange tool

Example 5.10:

Suppose we have a dataset of sales data for a small business, and we want to use PCA to understand which factors contribute the most to variations in sales. The dataset is as follows:

Store location	Advertising expense ($)	Product variety	Sales revenue ($)
Store A	5000	20	75,000
Store B	6000	15	80,000
Store C	4000	10	70,000
Store D	3000	30	85,000
Store E	7000	25	95,000

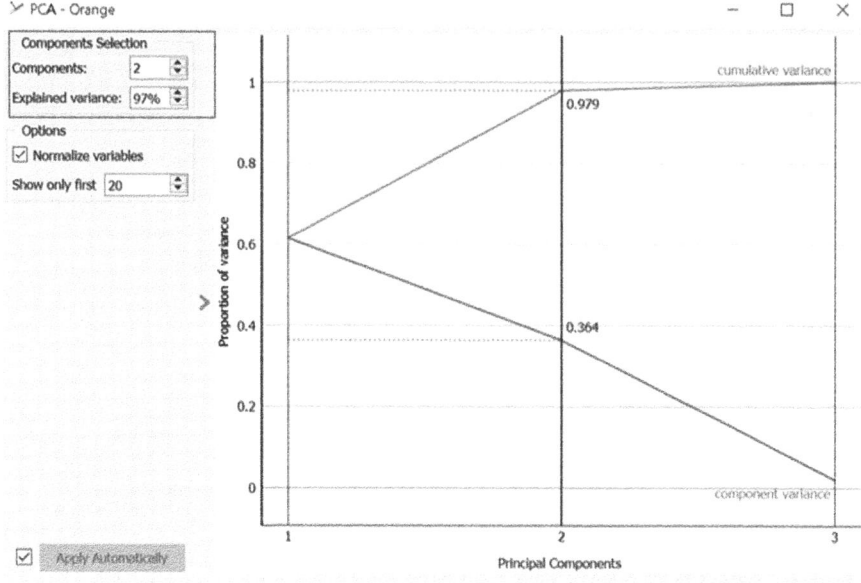

Fig. 5.48 Number of PCs

Data Table

Data instances: 2
Features: 3
Meta attributes: 2

	components	variance	Advertising Expense ($)	Product Variety	Sales Revenue ($)
1	PC1	0.615033	0.352646	0.592386	0.724375
2	PC2	0.364044	-0.833768	0.550345	-0.0441645

Fig. 5.49 Variance of PC1 and PC2

After following the steps of PCA, the number of components for the given example is 2, with the explained variance of 97% as shown in Fig. 5.48. (This outcome we get from PCA widget in Orange.)

The outcome of the two components (PC1 and PC2) from the Data Table widget is given in Fig. 5.49:

There are two levels of Data Analysis required for the outcome.

Level 1 is the Principal Component Analysis based on the outcomes obtained from Fig. 5.49:

PC1	PC2
Variance=0.615, indicating 61.50% of the total variance in data	Variance=0.364, indicating 36.40% of the total variance in data
PC1 is positively associated with all the three attributes, Advertising Expense ($), Product Variety, and Sales Revenue ($) are positive	PC2 is negatively associated with Advertising Expense and Sales Revenue, while it is positively associated with Product Variety

Level 2: The outcomes from the Save Data widget are as follows:

	PC1	PC2
Store location	Variance=0.615033	Variance=0.364044
Store A	−0.505241	0.0308041
Store B	−0.253728	−0.973582
Store C	−2.01339	−0.132269
Store D	0.675871	1.9369
Store E	2.09649	−0.86185

Substituting the values of PC1 and PC2 from the Level 2 outcome, we can devise the strategy and thus provide recommendations to the company as given below:

Store location	Value of PC1	Value of PC2	Strategy	Recommendations
Store A	−	+	Focus on successful strategies, while improve upon the negative values of PC1	Store has high negative score for PC1 and almost 0 for PC2. Should focus on increasing both advertising efforts and product variety
Store B	−	−	The company needs to work in all the listed attributes. More emphasis to be given to higher values of PCs	Should focus on all three attributes [Advertising Expense ($), Product Variety, and Sales Revenue ($)]
Store C	−	−	The company needs to work in all the listed attributes. More emphasis to be given to higher values of PCs	Should focus on all three attributes [Advertising Expense ($), Product Variety, and Sales Revenue ($)]
Store D	+	+	Continue its current strategy, no changes	No recommendations
Store E	+	−	Focus on successful strategies, while improve upon the negative values of PC2	Should focus on Advertising Expense

5.3.3   *Data Analytics Using Unstructured Data*

Data analytics with unstructured data includes extracting findings from non-tabular, non-structured data, such as text documents, images, social media postings, and videos. Unlike structured data, which blends perfectly into rows and columns, unstructured data is typically untidy, and needs tailored skills to analyze adequately.

Techniques like natural language processing (NLP) and image recognition are frequently used to handle unstructured data. For example, NLP can extract senti-ment, or named entities from text, while image recognition techniques may recog-nize objects, scenes, or even emotions from images.

Unstructured data analytics helps businesses acquire deeper insights into cus-tomer behavior, affinities, and demographics. For instance, researching customer reviews and social media interactions may disclose significant information that structured data alone could overlook, helping businesses optimize their products, customize marketing campaigns, and enhance the customer experience. As unstruc-tured data makes up the majority of the data created today, utilizing it efficiently may give a huge business advantage.

There are two types of unstructured data we will study, sentiment analysis and image analytics, as mentioned in Fig. 5.50.

Sentiment Analysis
Sentiment analysis in Orange entails using natural language processing (NLP) to analyze and classify emotions conveyed in text data, often categorizing sentiments as positive, negative, or neutral.

The steps of sentiment analysis in Orange tool involve five steps as mentioned below:

1. Corpus: This is the initial dataset of textual data to be studied.
2. Preprocess Text: In this step, the raw text is cleansed and prepared for analysis. This may involve deleting stop words, punctuation, and applying tokenization or stemming to simplify the text.
3. Tweet Profiler: This component presumably examines individual texts to find different properties, such as keywords, user information, or early classifications that might assist in sentiment analysis.
4. Sentiment Analysis: In this step, the texts are examined for their emotional tone, deciding whether the sentiment is good, negative, or neutral. This generally uses scoring algorithms or machine learning models constructed from sentiment data.

Fig. 5.50 Types of data analytics for unstructured data

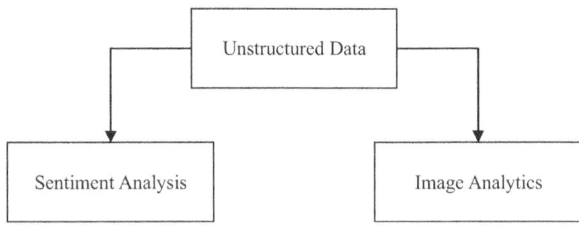

5. Distributions: After sentiment analysis, the findings are represented in the form of distributions. This helps to analyze the frequency and dispersion of sentiment scores in the data.

The steps are given in Fig. 5.51:
The outcomes of the distributions widget are given by Fig. 5.52:

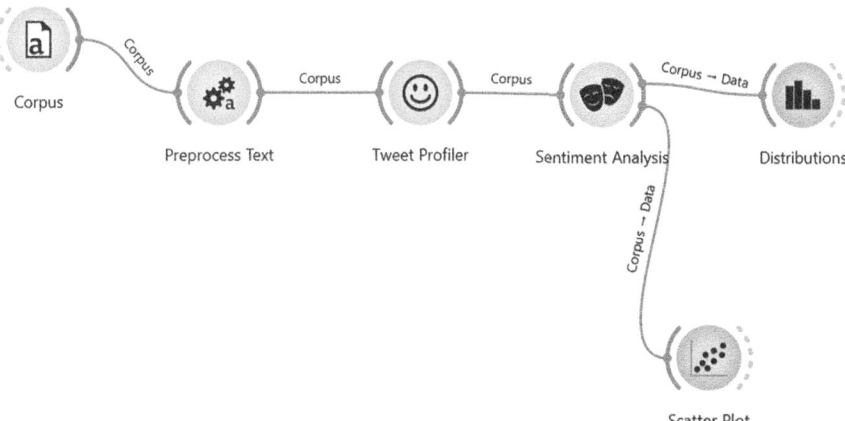

Fig. 5.51 Steps of sentiment analysis in Orange

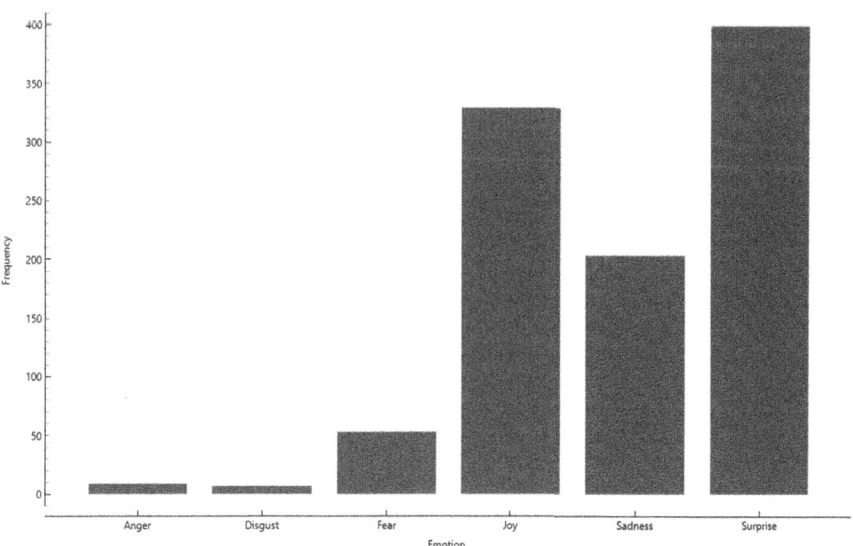

Fig. 5.52 Outcomes of the sentiments analysis in Orange

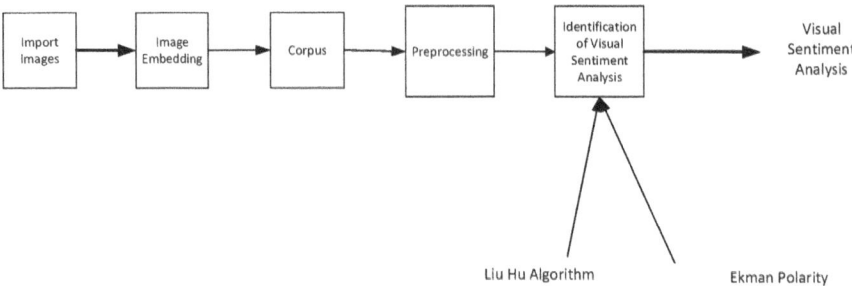

Fig. 5.53 Image analytics in Orange

Image Analytics

Earlier social media postings (on Facebook, Twitter) were text only, which were subsequently expanded to photos and videos, with specific platforms specialized to the publishing of images and videos (Instagram, Snapchat). There were a few notable observations:

- Tweets containing pictures are 34% more likely to be retweeted than tweets with no images (Webster, 2015),
- Instagram users post 55 million photographs a day to the platform (Bakhshi et al., 2014)
- Images on Facebook generate 53% more likes than the average post without images (Corliss, 2019)

These details show that image-based postings hold a stronger social media visibility than the text alone (Pittman & Reich, 2016). With the new technology and smart-phones, the future of social media will be more image based (Appel et al., 2019).

Image Analytics in Orange

The proposed model for image analytics is divided into three steps, as mentioned in Fig. 5.53. The first step of the model is image embedding, which takes the images and uses a predefined algorithm for a specific task. Image embedding requires evaluation of images where the vector representations are computed. The outcome of the image embedding algorithm is transferred to sentiment analysis algorithms which consist of a combination of Liu Hu Algorithm and Ekman Scoring.

5.4 Economic Implications of Data Analytics

In the preceding section, we discussed different types of predictive analytics and their consequences for business. In this part, we will analyze the economic implications associated with structured and unstructured data. For structured data, we will discuss both supervised learning techniques (such as regression and classification) and unsupervised learning approaches (such as clustering). For unstructured data, we will analyze the economic effects of sentiment analysis and image analytics. Each of these techniques delivers useful insights that increase the business's effectiveness, boost decision-making, and add to competitive edge.

5.4.1   Economic Implications of Structured Data

Structured data provides enormous economic advantages through the application of both supervised and unsupervised algorithms. Supervised learning approaches, such as linear regression and classification models, allow businesses to accurately predict outcomes. Unsupervised learning approaches, such as clustering, assist discover hidden trends, enabling businesses to target the specific segment.

Supervised Learning: Linear Regression
Linear regression is a technique for analyzing correlations between variables. Taking Eq. (5.1), the linear equation is given by

$$Y = b + aX$$

In businesses, the economic implications of linear regression can be used in two different ways to predict the *total cost* and *total revenue*.

If we need to estimate the total cost, Eq. (5.1) can be rewritten as

$$C = b + aQ$$

where C is the cost and Q is the quantity to be produced.
The total cost T_C interval $[Q1, Q2]$ is given by Eq. (5.10)

$$T_C = \int_{Q_1}^{Q_2} (b + aQ)dQ = b(Q_2 - Q_1) + a\left(\frac{Q_2^2}{2} - \frac{Q_1^2}{2}\right) \tag{5.10}$$

Equation (5.10) gives the total cost for producing between Q_1 and Q_2 units. Similarly, if we need to estimate total revenue, Eq. (5.1) can be rewritten as

$$R = b + aA$$

where R is the revenue and A is the advertising spend.
The total cost T_R interval $[A1, A2]$ is given by Eq. (5.11)

$$T_R = \int_{A_1}^{A_2} (b + aA)dA = b(A_2 - A_1) + a\left(\frac{A_2^2}{2} - \frac{A_1^2}{2}\right) \tag{5.11}$$

Equation (5.11) gives the total revenue for the advertisement spend between A_1 and A_2.

Supervised Learning: Classification Models

Classification models let businesses sort data into discrete groups based on features. These models have important economic consequences in fields such as finance (credit scoring), healthcare (disease detection), and marketing (customer segmentation). By precisely categorizing data, businesses can make more educated decisions, prevent risk, and optimize resources.

Profit Maximization

Consider a business employing a logistic regression classification model for predicting whether a consumer would react to a marketing effort (purchase or not). The model generates the probability $P(y = 1 \mid x)$ that a consumer y will purchase a product provided it has features x. Assuming the profit from a single marketing effort is p, the expected profit maximization $P(M)$ is given by Eq. (5.12):

$$P(M) = \int_0^1 p.P(y = 1 \mid x)dx \tag{5.12}$$

Expected Revenue

The expected revenue $E(R)$ from the marketing campaign can be estimated by integrating the probability distribution of customers identified as likely to purchase. Assuming the revenue from a single purchase is r, the estimated revenue across all customers is given by Eq. (5.13):

$$E(R) = \int_0^1 r.P(y = 1 \mid x)dx \tag{5.13}$$

Risk Reduction

In financial services, classification models are used to find creditworthiness of the borrower, by predicting whether the loan will be returned or not. If L is the default by predicting that the borrower has defaulted on the loan, then by integrating the probability distribution, we can identify the expected loss $E(L)$ as given by Eq. (5.14)

$$E(L) = \int_0^1 L.P(default \mid x)dx \tag{5.14}$$

5.4.2 *Economic Implications of Unstructured Data*

Businesses may benefit significantly from unstructured data, including text, images, and videos, but because of its complexity, the insights need sophisticated analytics. For example, sentiment analysis enables businesses to extract emotional nuances from social media postings, enabling businesses to assess public opinion and devise the strategies appropriately. Revenue growth, increased customer satisfaction, and loyalty might result from this. Similar to this, image analytics gives businesses the ability to examine visual information for trends and brand identification. Businesses may gain a competitive edge by using these types of analytics to unlock the unrealized potential of unstructured data.

Sentiment Analysis

Sentiment analysis has important economic implications, especially when it comes to assisting businesses in comprehending how customers feel and making better decisions.

Assume that a business's revenue $R(t)$ is a function of time t and that sentiment score $S(t)$, which is derived from customer feedback, influences the revenue. While negative sentiment may reduce revenue, excellent sentiment would increase customer engagement.

Assumptions for evaluating economic implications of Sentiment Analysis

- The sentiments can be scored as -1 for negative sentiment, 0 for neutral sentiment, and 1 for positive sentiment; thus, $S(t)\epsilon[-1, 1]$.
- Revenue is directly proportional to the sentiment score, $R(t)$ α $S(t)$.

As mentioned in the assumptions that $R(t)$ α $S(t)$, the rate of change of revenue $\frac{dR}{dt}$ can be denoted by Eq. (5.15)

$$\frac{dR(t)}{dt} = k.S(t) \tag{5.15}$$

where k is constant that measures the sensitivity of revenue to sentiment.

Over time T, the total revenue is given by Eq. (5.16)

$$R(T) = \int_{0}^{T} k.S(t)dt + R_0 \tag{5.16}$$

where R_0 is the initial revenue at $t = 0$.

As stated in the assumptions, the sentiment score ranges between -1, 0 and $+1$, following a sinusoidal waveform, which can be represented by Eq. (5.17)

$$S(t) = \sin\left(\frac{\pi t}{T}\right) \tag{5.17}$$

Thus, Eq. (X.XX) can be rewritten and mentioned by Eq. (5.18)

$$R(T) = \int_0^T k.\sin\left(\frac{\pi t}{T}\right) dt + R_0 \tag{5.18}$$

Upon elaboration, $R(T) = \frac{2kT}{\pi} + R_0$

The equation indicates that revenue is positively impacted by sentiment analysis, with revenue being proportional to $\frac{2kT}{\pi}$.

The integration demonstrates how sentiment analysis influences revenue over time. Positive sentiments boost revenue, while negative sentiments lessen it. Businesses may optimize their economic profits by constantly evaluating and modifying their strategy in response to customer sentiments. This technique enables a quantitative comprehension of the economic consequences of sentiment analysis.

Image Analytics

Image analytics has extensive implications in businesses, from devising marketing tactics to increasing product quality. Businesses that use image analytics may lower costs, streamline operations, and increase revenue.

Assume that a business's revenue $R(t)$ is influenced by the quality of image analytics $I(t)$.

Assumptions for evaluating economic implications of Image Analytics

- The sentiments can be scored as 0 for no use of image analytics or 1 optimal use of image analytics; thus, $I(t)\epsilon[0, 1]$.
- Revenue is directly proportional to image analytics, $R(t) \, \alpha \, I(t)$.

As mentioned in the assumptions that $R(t) \, \alpha \, I(t)$, the rate of change of revenue $\frac{dR}{dt}$ can be denoted by Eq. (5.19)

$$\frac{dR(t)}{dt} = k.I(t) \tag{5.19}$$

where k is constant that measures the sensitivity of revenue to image analytics.

Over time T, the total revenue is given by Eq. (5.20)

$$R(T) = \int_0^T k.I(t)dt + R_0 \tag{5.20}$$

where R_0 is the initial revenue at $t = 0$.

With the intervention of technology, image analytics will help businesses to grow exponentially, which can be represented by Eq. (5.21).

$$I(t) = 1 - e^{-\lambda t} \tag{5.21}$$

Thus, Eq. (5.21) can be rewritten and mentioned by Eq. (5.22)

$$R(T) = \int_0^T k.\left(1 - e^{-\lambda t}\right)dt + R_0 \tag{5.22}$$

Upon elaboration, $R(T) = kT - \frac{k}{\lambda}\left(1 - e^{-\lambda T}\right) + R_0$

As $T \to \infty$ (*long term*), $e^{-\lambda T} \to 0$, so, $R(T) = kT - \frac{k}{\lambda} + R_0$

The equation indicates that revenue grows linearly if image analytics are used by businesses for longer durations.

5.5 Conclusion

The use of data analytics in business has become vital, allowing businesses to harness structured and unstructured data to make data-driven decisions. Through structured data analysis, businesses may capture learning from historical data, analyze customer behavior, and forecast future trends, establishing a strategic edge. Supervised and unsupervised learning approaches extend this capability by identifying and anticipating outcomes.

Unstructured data analytics, notably sentiment and image analysis, adds an extra layer of knowledge that structured data alone cannot deliver. These approaches allow businesses to read customer reactions and visual signals from sources like social media and customer reviews.

The integration of such analytics in platforms like the Orange data mining tool gives businesses with concrete findings and practical processes, helping them to continuously react to evolving market conditions. Together, structured and unstructured data analytics offer a complete perspective of business data, creating comprehensive options that promote sustained performance.

Exercise

Exercise 1: Understanding the Role of Data Analytics in Business

A consulting firm, ABC Solutions, has been contracted by a small retail company, XYZ, to enhance its business decision-making and operational efficiency using data analytics. XYZ, which runs both online and offline businesses, has faced changing revenues, retention of customers issues, and excessive stocks of some merchandise.

To stay competitive, the company's leadership wants to employ data analytics for a deeper understanding of customer behavior, handling of inventory, and promotional activities.

XYZ's key purpose is to understand how data analytics may be used throughout its operations to improve decision-making and boost profitability. The consulting company, ABC Solutions, will develop a report showcasing how prominent businesses in diverse sectors have effectively used data analytics to meet comparable business challenges. This study will serve as an outline for XYZ, emphasizing how data analytics may enable more accurate forecasting, targeted marketing, and efficient inventory.

ABC Solutions will present a detailed study explaining the importance of data analytics in current business operations, notably focused on decision-making. The work will cover case studies from three successful businesses that have successfully implemented data analytics:

1. *Amazon: Known for its superior data analytics in demand forecasting and recommendation systems, Amazon has improved its supply chain and tailored consumer experience.*
2. *Netflix: Through data-driven suggestions and content strategy, Netflix has greatly boosted user engagement and happiness, growing its worldwide subscriber base.*
3. *Starbucks: Leveraging data analytics for site selection, customer loyalty, and product customization, Starbucks tailors its products to local demand and fosters customer loyalty.*

Preparing the business report will conclude with practical insights and suggestions on how XYZ may use comparable techniques to achieve quantifiable gains in profitability, efficiency, and customer engagement.

Exercise 2: Identifying Types of Data

A financial services business, 123 Capital, is undertaking digital transformation to increase its data management and analytics capabilities. At present, data inside 123 Capital is maintained across numerous forms, leading to concerns when it involves analysis, reporting, and compliance with regulations. The company decided to begin an initiative to categorize and arrange data across departments so they can effectively apply data analytics.

The objective is to train employees about various forms of data—structured, semi-structured, and unstructured—and assist them understand how each may be successfully employed in data analytics.

The report needs to include concrete instances on how 123 Capital may store, process, and analyze each data type for improving comprehensive data-driven decision-making.

Exercise 3: Utilizing Predictive Analytics

A retail chain, PQR Retail, has been facing variable demand across its outlets and is sometimes hindered by inventory issues (surplus stock or stockouts) during peak seasons. PQR Retail anticipates solving this by using predictive analytics to boost demand forecasting, which will help the business manage inventory levels.

PQR Retail wants to apply predictive analytics to project future demand for each product category based on previous sales data, seasonal trends, and external influences.

You are required to write a report that will be created to outline the processes, predictive model, and detailed analysis for estimating demand and managing inventory effectively.

Sample Dataset

Date	Store_ ID	Product_ Category	Sales_ Volume	Price	Promotion	Holiday	Weather
1/1/ 2024	101	Electronics	25	200	Yes	No	Cloudy
1/1/ 2024	102	Apparel	40	50	No	No	Sunny
1/1/ 2024	103	Groceries	75	10	No	No	Rainy
1/2/ 2024	101	Electronics	20	200	Yes	No	Sunny
1/2/ 2024	102	Apparel	35	45	Yes	No	Cloudy
1/2/ 2024	103	Groceries	70	10	No	No	Sunny
1/3/ 2024	101	Electronics	30	190	No	No	Rainy
1/3/ 2024	102	Apparel	25	48	No	No	Sunny
1/3/ 2024	103	Groceries	60	10	Yes	No	Cloudy
1/4/ 2024	101	Electronics	28	200	Yes	No	Cloudy
1/4/ 2024	102	Apparel	45	50	No	No	Rainy
1/4/ 2024	103	Groceries	65	10	No	No	Sunny
1/5/ 2024	101	Electronics	18	205	No	No	Sunny
1/5/ 2024	102	Apparel	30	52	Yes	No	Cloudy
1/5/ 2024	103	Groceries	55	10	No	No	Rainy

(continued)

Date	Store_ ID	Product_ Category	Sales_ Volume	Price	Promotion	Holiday	Weather
1/6/ 2024	101	Electronics	22	200	Yes	No	Cloudy
1/6/ 2024	102	Apparel	40	50	No	No	Sunny
1/6/ 2024	103	Groceries	80	10	No	No	Cloudy
1/7/ 2024	101	Electronics	26	195	No	Yes	Rainy
1/7/ 2024	102	Apparel	35	45	Yes	Yes	Cloudy
1/7/ 2024	103	Groceries	90	10	No	Yes	Rainy
1/8/ 2024	101	Electronics	32	200	Yes	No	Sunny
1/8/ 2024	102	Apparel	50	48	No	No	Sunny
1/8/ 2024	103	Groceries	85	10	No	No	Cloudy
1/9/ 2024	101	Electronics	29	190	No	No	Rainy
1/9/ 2024	102	Apparel	45	50	Yes	No	Sunny
1/9/ 2024	103	Groceries	78	10	Yes	No	Sunny
1/10/ 2024	101	Electronics	20	210	No	No	Cloudy
1/10/ 2024	102	Apparel	40	55	No	No	Rainy
1/10/ 2024	103	Groceries	72	10	No	No	Cloudy

Exercise 4

A consumer electronics company is trying to achieve competitive advantage and understood that customer perceptions, brand image, and product quality reviews on social media and also images posted on social media have substantial economic implications for revenue. The company was using structured data analysis for sales analysis, lately understood to study the unstructured data and capture the reviews and opinions from social media as well.

The data obtained are as follows:

Sentiment Analysis:

- Initial Revenue, $R_0 = 100{,}000$
- Sensitivity constant, $k = 5000$
- Total Time, $T = 12$ months

Image Analytics

- Initial Revenue, $R_0 = 100{,}000$
- Sensitivity constant, $k = 3000$
- Decay rate, $\lambda = 0.1$
- Total Time, $T = 12$ months

Map out a comprehensive revenue trajectory influenced by unstructured data for the company.

Hint:

For Sentiment Analysis:

Using Eq. (5.18), we get

$$R(T) = \int_0^T k.\sin\left(\frac{\pi t}{T}\right) dt + R_0 \approx 119{,}098$$

For Image Analytics:

Using Eq. (5.22), we get

$$R(T) = \int_0^T k.\left(1 - e^{-\lambda t}\right) dt + R_0 \approx 156{,}964$$

Thus, combined revenue from sentiment analysis and Image Analytics can be given as:

$$R_{total} = 119{,}098 + 156{,}964 = 276{,}062$$

References

Ansari, Y. (2023, June 14). Understanding logistic regression: A beginner's guide. *Medium*. https://medium.com/@novus_afk/understanding-logistic-regression-a-beginners-guide-73f148866910

Appel, G., Grewal, L., Hadi, R., & Stephen, A. T. (2019). The future of social media in marketing. *Journal of the Academy of Marketing Science*. https://doi.org/10.1007/s11747-019-00695-1

Aydiner, A. S., Tatoglu, E., Bayraktar, E., Zaim, S., & Delen, D. (2019). Business analytics and firm performance: The mediating role of business process performance. *Journal of Business Research, 96*(C), 228–237. https://ideas.repec.org//a/eee/jbrese/v96y2019icp228-237.html

Baeldung. (2020, October 7). *Multiclass classification using support vector machines*. https://www.baeldung.com/cs/svm-multiclass-classification

Bakhshi, S., Shamma, D. A., & Gilbert, E. (2014). Faces engage us: Photos with faces attract more likes and comments on Instagram. *Proceedings of the SIGCHI Conference on Human Factors in Computing Systems*, 965–974. https://doi.org/10.1145/2556288.2557403

Corliss, R. (2019). *Photos on Facebook generate 53% more likes than the average post*. https://blog.hubspot.com/blog/tabid/6307/bid/33800/photos-on-facebook-generate-53-more-likes-than-the-average-post-new-data.aspx

Datatron. (2021). What is a support vector machine? *Datatron*. https://datatron.com/what-is-a-support-vector-machine/

Evidently AI. (2024). *How to interpret a confusion matrix for a machine learning model*. https://www.evidentlyai.com/classification-metrics/confusion-matrix

Guo, J., & Li, L. (2022). Exploring the relationship between social commerce features and consumers' repurchase intentions: The mediating role of perceived value. *Frontiers in Psychology, 12*, 775056. https://doi.org/10.3389/fpsyg.2021.775056

Mallick, C. B. (2023). *Principal component analysis working and applications | Spiceworks—Spiceworks*. https://www.spiceworks.com/tech/big-data/articles/what-is-principal-component-analysis/

Pittman, M., & Reich, B. (2016). Social media and loneliness: Why an Instagram picture may be worth more than a thousand Twitter words. *Computers in Human Behavior, 62*, 155–167. https://doi.org/10.1016/j.chb.2016.03.084

PredictiveAnalyticsToday. (2024). *Orange Data mining in 2024*. PAT RESEARCH: B2B Reviews, Buying Guides & Best Practices. https://www.predictiveanalyticstoday.com/orange-data-mining/

Smith, S., & McConnell, S. (2024). The use of artificial neural networks and decision trees: Implications for health-care research. *Open Computer Science, 14*. https://doi.org/10.1515/comp-2022-0279

TutorialRide. (2022). *K-means clustering in data mining*. https://www.tutorialride.com/data-mining/k-means-clustering-in-data-mining.htm

Webster. (2015). *8 Suprising Twitter statistics to get more engagement* [Postcorn]. Postcron – Social Media Marketing Blog and Digital Marketing Blog. https://postcron.com/en/blog/8-surprising-twitter-statistics-get-more-engagement/

Wissuchek, C., & Zschech, P. (2024). Prescriptive analytics systems revised: A systematic literature review from an information systems perspective. *Information Systems and E-Business Management*. https://doi.org/10.1007/s10257-024-00688-w

Wolniak, R., & Grebski, W. (2023). Functioning of predictive analytics in business. *Scientific Papers of Silesian University of Technology Organization and Management Series, 2023*. https://doi.org/10.29119/1641-3466.2023.175.40

Index

The manufacturer's authorised representative in the EU is Springer
Nature Customer Service Centre GmbH, Europaplatz 3, 69115 Heidelberg,
Germany. If you have any concerns regarding our products, please
contact ProductSafety@springernature.com

Printed and bound by CPI Group (UK) Ltd, Croydon, CR0 4YY

27/04/2026

02097572-0014